CONTENTS

GREAT ACHIEVERS

LIVES OF THE PHYSICALLY CHALLENGED

JIM ABBOTT
baseball star

LUDWIG VAN BEETHOVEN
composer

LOUIS BRAILLE
inventor

CHRIS BURKE
actor

JULIUS CAESAR
Roman emperor

ROY CAMPANELLA
baseball star

RAY CHARLES
musician

ROBERT DOLE
politician

STEPHEN HAWKING
physicist

JACKIE JOYNER-KERSEE
champion athlete

HELEN KELLER
humanitarian

RON KOVIC
antiwar activist

MARIO LEMIEUX
ice hockey star

MARLEE MATLIN
actress

JOHN MILTON
poet

MARY TYLER MOORE
actress

FLANNERY O'CONNOR
author

ITZHAK PERLMAN
violinist

FRANKLIN D. ROOSEVELT
U.S. president

HENRI DE TOULOUSE-LAUTREC
artist

STEVIE WONDER
musician

CHRIS BURKE

OILERS

GREAT ACHIEVERS

LIVES OF THE PHYSICALLY CHALLENGED

ACTOR

Helen Monsoon Geraghty

Chelsea House Publishers

Philadelphia

CHELSEA HOUSE PUBLISHERS

EDITORIAL DIRECTOR Richard Rennert
EXECUTIVE MANAGING EDITOR Karyn Gullen Browne
COPY CHIEF Robin James
PICTURE EDITOR Adrian G. Allen
ART DIRECTOR Robert Mitchell
MANUFACTURING DIRECTOR Gerald Levine

GREAT ACHIEVERS: LIVES OF THE PHYSICALLY CHALLENGED

SENIOR EDITOR Kathy Kuhtz Campbell
SERIES DESIGN Basia Niemczyc

Staff for **CHRIS BURKE**
ASSOCIATE EDITOR Martin Schwabacher
COPY EDITOR Joy Sanchez
EDITORIAL ASSISTANT Kelsey Goss
PICTURE RESEARCHER Wendy P. Wills
DESIGN ASSISTANT Lydia Rivera
COVER ILLUSTRATION Richard Martin

3 5 7 9 8 6 4

Library of Congress Cataloging-in-Publication Data

Geraghty, Helen Monsoon.
Chris Burke / Helen Monsoon Geraghty.
p. cm.—(Great achievers)
Includes bibliographical references and index.
Summary: Examines the life of a young man with Down syndrome who fulfilled his dream of becoming a television star.
ISBN 0-7910-2081-9.
0-7910-2094-0 (pbk.)
1. Burke, Chris, 1965- —Juvenile literature. 2. Handicapped in television—Juvenile literature. 3. Television actors and actresses—United States—Biography—Juvenile literature. 4. Life goes on (Television program)—Juvenile literature. [1. Burke, Chris, 1965- . 2. Actors and actresses. 3. Down's syndrome. 4. Mentally handicapped.] I. Title. II. Series. III. Series: Great achievers (Chelsea House Publishers)
PN2287.B79G47 1994 93-4833
791.45'028'092—dc20 CIP
[B] AC

FRONTISPIECE:

Chris Burke speaks with teenagers at a convention of the Canadian Down Syndrome Association in Toronto, Canada, in June 1990.

A Message for Everyone

Jerry Lewis

Just 44 years ago—when I was the ripe old age of 23—an incredible stroke of fate rocketed me to overnight stardom as an entertainer. After the initial shock wore off, I began to have a very strong feeling that, in return for all life had given me, I must find a way of giving something back. At just that moment, a deeply moving experience in my personal life persuaded me to take up the leadership of a fledgling battle to defeat a then little-known group of diseases called muscular dystrophy, as well as other related neuromuscular diseases—all of which are disabling and, in the worst cases, cut life short.

In 1950, when the Muscular Dystrophy Association (MDA)—of which I am national chairman—was established, physical disability was looked on as a matter of shame. Franklin Roosevelt, who guided America through World War II from a wheelchair, and Harold Russell, the World War II hero who lost both hands in battle, then became an Academy Award–winning movie star and chairman of the President's Committee on Employment of the Handicapped, were the exceptions. One of the reasons that muscular dystrophy and related diseases were so little known was that people who had been disabled by them were hidden at home, away from the pity and discomfort with which they were generally regarded by society. As I got to know and began working with people who have disabilities, I quickly learned what a tragic mistake this perception was. And my determination to correct this terrible problem soon became as great as my commitment to see disabling neuromuscular diseases wiped from the face of the earth.

I have long wondered why it never occurs to us, as we experience the knee-jerk inclination to feel sorry for people who are physically disabled, that lives such as those led by President Roosevelt, Harold Russell, and all of the extraordinary people profiled in this Great Achievers series demonstrate unmistakably how wrong we are. Physical disability need not be something that blights life and destroys opportunity for personal fulfillment and accomplishment. On the contrary, as people such as Ray Charles, Stephen Hawking, and Ron Kovic prove, physical disability can be a spur to greatness rather than a condemnation of emptiness.

In fact, if my experience with physically disabled people can be taken as a guide, as far as accomplishment is concerned, they have a slight edge on the rest of us. The unusual challenges they face require finding greater-than-average sources of energy and determination to achieve much of what able-bodied people take for granted. Often, this ultimately translates into a lifetime of superior performance in whatever endeavor people with disabilities choose to pursue.

If you have watched my Labor Day Telethon over the years, you know exactly what I am talking about. Annually, we introduce to tens of millions of Americans people whose accomplishments would distinguish them regardless of their physical conditions—top-ranking executives, physicians, scientists, lawyers, musicians, and artists. The message I hope the audience receives is not that these extraordinary individuals have achieved what they have by overcoming a dreadful disadvantage that the rest of us are lucky not to have to endure. Rather, I hope our viewers reflect on the fact that these outstanding people have been ennobled and strengthened by the tremendous challenges they have faced.

In 1992, MDA, which has grown over the past four decades into one of the world's leading voluntary health agencies, established a personal achievement awards program to demonstrate to the nation that the distinctive qualities of people with disabilities are by no means confined to the famous. What could have been more appropriate or timely in that year of the implementation of the 1990 Americans with Disabilities Act than to take an action that could perhaps finally achieve the alteration of public perception of disability, which MDA had struggled over four decades to achieve?

On Labor Day, 1992, it was my privilege to introduce to America MDA's inaugural national personal achievement award winner, Steve Mikita, assistant attorney general of the state of Utah. Steve graduated magna cum laude from Duke University as its first wheelchair student in history and was subsequently named the outstanding young lawyer of the year by the Utah Bar Association. After he spoke on the Telethon with an eloquence that caused phones to light up from coast to coast, people asked me where he had been all this time and why they had not known of him before, so deeply impressed were they by him. I answered that he and thousands like him have been here all along. We just have not adequately *noticed* them.

It is my fervent hope that we can eliminate indifference once and for all and make it possible for all of our fellow citizens with disabilities to gain their rightfully high place in our society.

On Facing Challenges

John Callahan

I was paralyzed for life in 1972, at the age of 21. A friend and I were driving in a Volkswagen on a hot July night, when he smashed the car at full speed into a utility pole. He suffered only minor injuries. But my spinal cord was severed during the crash, leaving me without any feeling from my diaphragm downward. The only muscles I could move were some in my upper body and arms, and I could also extend my fingers. After spending a lot of time in physical therapy, it became possible for me to grasp a pen.

I've always loved to draw. When I was a kid, I made pictures of everything from Daffy Duck (one of my lifelong role models) to caricatures of my teachers and friends. I've always been a people watcher, it seems; and I've always looked at the world in a sort of skewed way. Everything I see just happens to translate immediately into humor. And so, humor has become my way of coping. As the years have gone by, I have developed a tremendous drive to express my humor by drawing cartoons.

The key to cartooning is to put a different spin on the expected, the normal. And that's one reason why many of my cartoons deal with the disabled: amputees, quadriplegics, paraplegics, the blind. The public is not used to seeing them in cartoons.

But there's another reason why my subjects are often disabled men and women. I'm sick and tired of people who presume to speak for the disabled. Call me a cripple, call me a gimp, call me paralyzed for life.

Just don't call me something I'm not. I'm not "differently abled," and my cartoons show that disabled people should not be treated any differently than anyone else.

All of the men, women, and children who are profiled in the Great Achievers series share this in common: their various handicaps have not prevented them from accomplishing great things. Their life stories are worth knowing about because they have found the strength and courage to develop their talents and to follow their dreams as fully as they can.

Whether able-bodied or disabled, a person must strive to overcome obstacles. There's nothing greater than to see a person who faces challenges and conquers them, regardless of his or her limitations.

The Burke family (from left to right, Marian, J. R., Anne, Ellen, Chris, and Frank) created a loving, supportive environment that encouraged Chris to develop his talents to the fullest.

1

“Forget That Stuff”

AT THE RECEPTION after graduation from the Don Guanella special boarding school in 1986, Chris Burke and his classmates were talking about their plans. Some of them had jobs in small-town businesses, others were going to work for their parents, but when people asked Chris what he would be doing after graduation, he told them that he was planning to go to Hollywood to become a star.

His parents, Frank and Marian Burke, cringed. At birth Chris had been labeled “mongoloid,” a condition now known as Down syndrome. This meant that Chris had 47 chromosomes in each cell, rather than the usual 46, and would probably have a low I.Q., speech and hearing problems, flaccid muscles, stunted growth, and the characteristic “mongoloid” face with flat features and slanted eyes. (John Langdon Down, the London doctor who first described “mongoloids” in 1866, was struck by their physical resemblance to the residents of Mongolia.) The Burkes' family doctor told them that Chris would never walk or talk, and she urged them to institutionalize him before he could blight the lives of their three other children.

Frank and Marian never considered putting Chris in a residential facility. They took him home and, when Chris was slow to crawl, they got down on the floor and showed him how. When he was slow to talk, they bombarded him with language, foreshadowing infant stimulation programs that schools would develop a decade later. When they found that special classes in New York City public schools were not challenging enough for him, they searched out the best private schools available at the time: the Kennedy Child Study Center in New York City; Cardinal Cushing School and Training Center in Hanover, Massachusetts, near Boston; and finally the Don Guanella school, run by Catholic priests in Springfield, Pennsylvania, outside Philadelphia. At all his schools Chris was an important figure, greeting visitors, hosting talent nights, and writing and filming videos. His feelings about himself were so positive that one day, when he saw a United Parcel Service truck, he decided to change the name of his syndrome. "The truck said UPS on the side," he later recalled. "I really liked that. I decided it stood for UP Syndrome." After that, he said he had Up syndrome, not Down. But the grim truth was that in 1986 a person with Down syndrome would be lucky to get a job as a waiter in a fast-food restaurant or as a packer on an assembly line.

The staff at Don Guanella, like Chris's parents, did not seem pleased about his plans. Many students fantasized about being rock singers or basketball stars, and as a result one of the school's main jobs was to help them develop realistic goals. Classes went to shopping malls and fast-food restaurants where students could observe the kinds of jobs they would probably have someday. By graduation everyone in Chris's class had a practical goal except him.

When the reception was over and Chris and his parents returned to their car, he lay down exhausted in the backseat. As he closed his eyes, he could hear his parents talking about his future. "Dear," Marian said grimly to Frank, "this really is the first day of the rest of our lives."

That June, Chris returned to his old summer job in Point Lookout, Long Island, a tiny beachfront town where his

Chris spent several summers doing maintenance work in Point Lookout, Long Island, where his family lived in the summer.

family owned a vacation house. He got up at 6:00 each morning, made himself breakfast, and went to the town park, where he swept the walks and checked the beach and ballfield for trash and then positioned himself next to the maintenance shack to help people check out athletic equipment.

His first year on the job, when he was 18, he was harassed by anonymous phone calls. One night someone tipped over the maintenance shack and destroyed it. Chris's older brother, Frank junior, known in the family as J. R., figured out that the culprits were some of the other boys who worked in maintenance. J. R. went to the park,

Folksingers John and Joe DeMasi met Chris at a summer camp for disabled children and teenagers in Lido Beach, Long Island. Chris participated in their music and drama programs and helped to organize talent shows. John DeMasi said of Chris, "I laugh when he's called handicapped because he's more advanced than a lot of people I know, people who are always complaining about their lives. Chris handles life great."

found the boys, and told them that he was Chris's brother and that he had a really short temper. Frank Burke talked to the head of maintenance, who called a meeting of the staff and said that it took little minds to pick on someone like Chris. After that the trouble stopped.

But now, in his third year on the job, Chris found it dull because after making his rounds in the morning, he had nothing to do except sit in the sun and listen to music. After work he visited the Anchor Program, a camp for handicapped children and teenagers in nearby Lido Beach, Long Island, where he was friendly with John and Joe DeMasi, two professional folksingers who ran the music and drama programs. They treated him almost as if he were one of the staff and let him help organize talent shows, where he break-danced and "moonwalked," but he had been doing this since he was 13.

Chris spent evenings writing television scripts, because two years earlier he had realized that there was no one like him on his favorite television shows, such as "Growing Pains" and "Little House on the Prairie." He had not actually believed that these scripts would be successful until he saw a television listing for an episode of "The Fall Guy" that featured a boy with Down syndrome, 10-year-old Jason Kingsley. In the episode Jason's character was mainstreamed in a regular school, spoke foreign languages, and participated in the Special Olympics. Most important from Chris's point of view, Jason had a starring role on television.

Chris obtained Jason's address from the local television station and wrote him a fan letter that was answered by Jason's mother, Emily Kingsley, a writer for "Sesame Street." She told Chris that Jason was no novice on television, having been a regular on "Sesame Street," the star of a special "This Is My Son," and a guest on "Donahue," "Good Morning America," and a dozen other talk shows.

After Emily Kingsley and Chris became pen pals, she invited him to her annual summer picnic in Westchester

County, New York, where she was impressed by his slenderness. Hypotonia, poor muscle development, makes it difficult for people with Down syndrome to exercise and, consequently, they tend to be obese. Kingsley was also struck by how handsome Chris was. (Attractiveness was a family trait: both his brother, J. R., and his two sisters, Anne and Ellen, had appeared in television and print advertisements when they were young.) She was also impressed by Chris's clear pronunciation; although he had a narrow mouth and poor muscle development in his tongue, like other people with Down syndrome, years of practicing to be an actor and taking speech therapy had made him unusually articulate.

In one of her letters, Emily Kingsley asked Chris what he wanted to do after graduation from Don Guanella. When he responded that he wanted to be an actor, she did not think he was being overoptimistic but wrote back that, though television did not have many roles for people with Down syndrome, if such a role came up, Chris would be a natural for it. After getting Kingsley's letter, Chris wrote scripts with passion, sitting up past midnight filling long yellow pads.

His writing made his family miserable. They were pleased that Chris had enough self-confidence to write for television, but his scripts tended to follow existing episodes of his favorite TV programs—with only one difference, the addition of a person with Down syndrome. It was hard to see how this kind of writing would get him anywhere.

One day, when he and J. R. were sitting around the Point Lookout house, talking about Chris's dreams, J. R. lost his temper. "Forget that stuff," J. R. yelled. "Be realistic. Get a job." Chris looked away from his brother and told him to stop shouting. It was a difficult situation because, though J. R. loved Chris, he thought he was throwing his life away, while Chris was sure that someday he would be a star.

In the fall of 1986, Chris returned with his parents to Manhattan, where they lived in Peter Cooper Village, a development on the East Side. Peter Cooper Village had many parks and playgrounds, but it was no Point Lookout.

In 1981, Chris and his family visited his sister Anne and her children, Sara (top) and Nora, in Poland. Chris is devoted to Nora, who has Rett syndrome, a degenerative disease that left her unable to walk or talk.

Buildings were high-rise, doors were locked, and during school hours there were only toddlers in the playgrounds.

Frank and Marian set up a number of interviews for Chris for jobs as a messenger or stock boy. He wore his best suit and arrived punctually for appointments, but frequently the person who was supposed to interview him had mysteriously disappeared, or Chris was sent on a wild-goose chase from one department to another. After a while he understood—nobody wanted to hire someone with Down syndrome.

Chris ran out of job prospects and had nothing to do except spend his time idly. In the mornings he shot baskets in the playgrounds and rambled through the parks of Peter Cooper Village. Later, he drifted over to the record and video stores on 14th Street, where he checked out as many as 10 movies at a time. Afternoons he baby-sat for his sister Ellen's children, Sara and Nora, who lived on the other side of Peter Cooper Village. Nora, who was six, had Rett syndrome, a degenerative neurological disease, and could neither walk nor talk. Chris loved to cuddle her against his chest and tickle her to make her laugh. Because she could not dance, he loved to dance for her.

Ellen, Nora's mother, enrolled Chris in a job training program she found a few blocks away from her house. When he attended, however, he found that the teachers were not accustomed to people with Down syndrome and did not realize that, though he might forget instructions at first, he could master them through repetition; nor did they realize that, though he might do odd or inappropriate things at first, in time he would master classroom protocol. Within days he was demoted from the training program to a sheltered workshop at the same location.

In this workshop, which Chris soon realized was not sheltered at all, 20 people sat in a cavernous room, stuffing small items into bags and boxes. No one was allowed to talk except for a supervisor who barked orders. "I hated it," Chris remembered. "They wouldn't let me talk or do anything." When Ellen came to visit Chris, she was shocked by what she saw. A supervisor was yelling at Chris, and he was frightened and confused. "It was like something out of *One Flew Over the Cuckoo's Nest* [a novel by Ken Kesey, and later a film starring Jack Nicholson, in which patients in a mental hospital are terrorized by a brutish nurse]. I never, ever saw Chris behave the way he behaved around her. He was acting retarded. We got him out of there really fast." It was a frightening example of how the behavior of people with Down syndrome—even someone as gifted as Chris—can be affected by the low expectations of others.

Chris probably would have gone back to shooting baskets and renting videos, but Ellen had another idea. Nora attended P.S. 138, a school for special children with branches all over the city. Nora's classroom was located at 400 First Avenue, only a few blocks away from her home. Ellen reasoned that because Chris had a talent for baby-sitting Nora, he might be good at caring for other handicapped children. She asked Nora's teacher, Tom Roeder, if Chris could volunteer in his classroom.

P.S. 138 had no volunteer program, but Roeder asked Chris to come in for an interview. When Chris described how he cared for Nora, Roeder said he could feel the love between the two. A few days later, when Roeder visited Ellen's apartment and Chris showed him how he lifted Nora gently and positioned her carefully so as to avoid hurting her, Roeder told Chris that even he could learn a thing or two from him.

The news that Chris had been accepted as a volunteer thrilled his parents, especially his mother, who believed that he would have an opportunity to improve his social skills. At first, the job proved to be difficult for Chris because the children in Nora's class were severely retarded. Some of them had not had proper exercise when they were young and consequently they were spastic; their muscles twitched uncontrollably. Others had never had dental work and had oversize teeth that stuck out at odd angles. Some of the children drooled. Initially, Chris clung to Nora for comfort, but after a few weeks he began to move around the class, hugging the children and rubbing their arms. He learned all of their names, and soon their faces brightened when they saw him enter the room.

Chris horses around with Tom Roeder, a teacher at P.S. 138, a public school for disabled youth in New York City. When Roeder saw how well Burke interacted with his niece Nora, who was in Roeder's class, he accepted Burke as a volunteer.

Outside the classroom Chris had difficulty getting along with the other staff members. At Don Guanella there had been a lot of hugging, but here he found that when he played his favorite trick of walking up behind colleagues and hugging them without warning, they did not always appreciate it. In fact, sometimes they were offended. When staff members complained about his physicality or made fun of his lapses in judgment, it reminded him of the bad old days in Point Lookout. Gradually, though, Chris learned to give people time to know him and eventually he learned how to accept criticism gracefully.

Tom Roeder became his first friend at P.S. 138. He and Chris went to lunch together, ordering the same meal every time: bacon, eggs, and french fries. They joked that they must be brothers because they both had fair skin and reddish hair and they talked about their families, which were warm, loving, and supportive. Fridays, after work, the staff of P.S. 138 usually got together for a few beers. When they invited Chris to join them, he finally had friends his own age.

Chris, however, kept pursuing his dream, watching as many movies as possible, memorizing casts, noting ideas, and writing scripts. At P.S. 138 he announced that his goals were to be an actor by the age of 23, to have his own television show, and to star in movies. "He expressed his dreams really well," said Roeder—so well that "people thought he was nuts."

Jim Gillis, a P.S. 138 father and veteran actor, supported Chris's aspirations, loaning Chris tapes of his own performances in *Tiger Warsaw* and other movies, which Chris watched over and over again. When Chris asked Gillis how to break into show business, Gillis told him that with his charm and expressiveness he had a realistic chance of becoming an actor. Gillis explained that there was no "how" to acting; if Chris could share his emotions and his energy with others, he could succeed. After this discussion Chris worked so hard writing scripts and studying old movies that his father complained that he was not getting enough sleep.

Then one night in December 1986, Chris was watching television in his room when his mother called to him from the kitchen. As Chris walked into the kitchen, he saw Marian holding the phone, looking puzzled. "Christopher," she said, "this lady wants to know if you would like to try out for a part in a movie for television."

"Yes," he said. "Yes, yes! I'm going to be in a movie."

The woman on the phone was a Warner Brothers casting director who had first called Emily Kingsley, asking Jason to audition for a role in a TV drama. When it became apparent that Jason was too young for the part, Kingsley had recommended Chris, along with many other young men with Down syndrome.

Marian tried to warn Chris, who was beside himself with delight, that an audition was no guarantee of a part, but he was too excited to listen. "I waited for this chance all my life," he said. "I didn't know if I would get it. But I wanted it so bad."

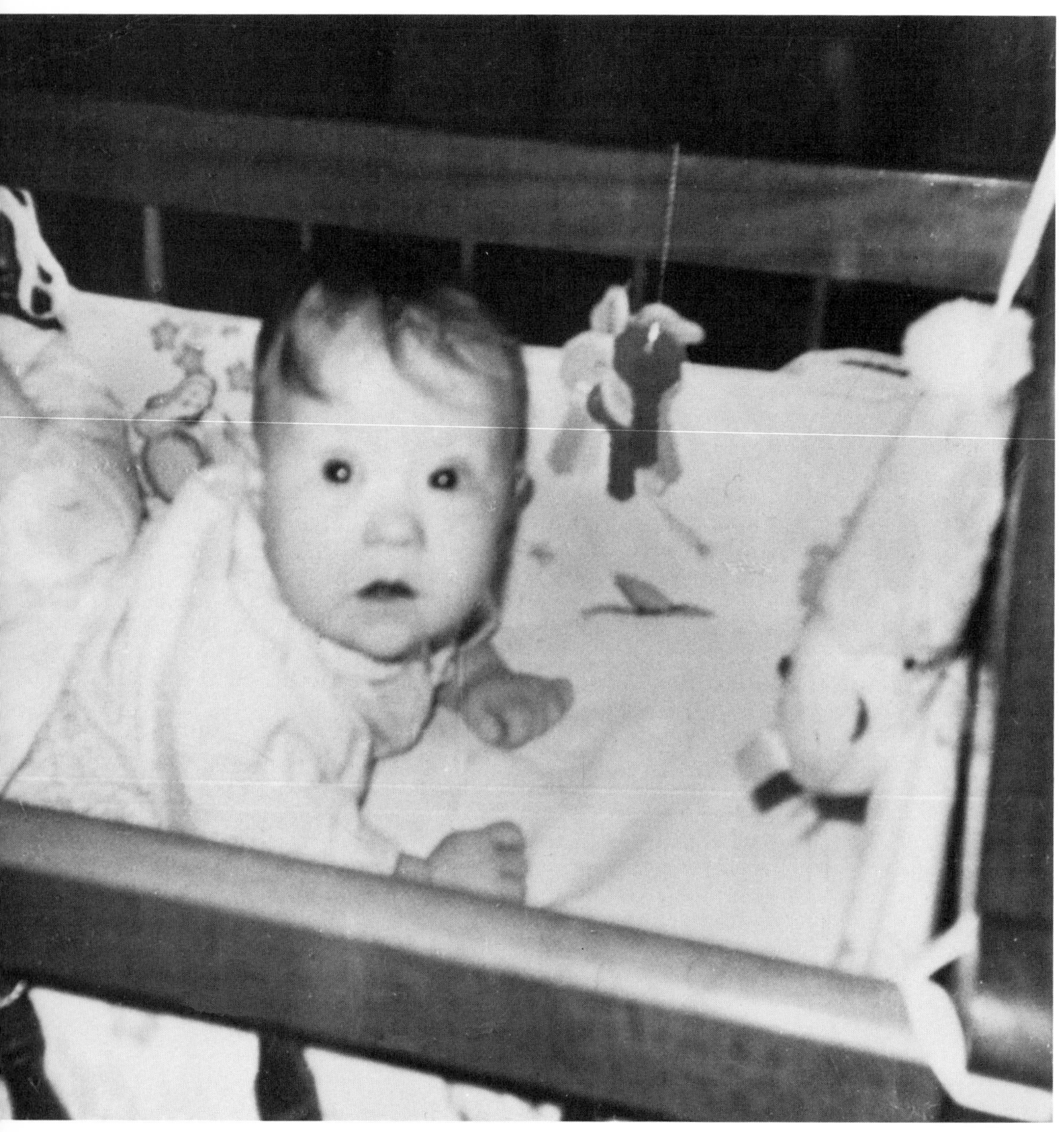

Chris, shown here at age three months, was always loved and fully accepted by his family. His parents did not tell Chris's siblings about his disability for several months and encouraged them to play with him as they would any other baby.

2

"Put This Child Away"

WHEN CHRIS WAS BORN on August 26, 1965, at St. Vincent's Hospital in Manhattan, he was a lively, handsome baby, weighing seven pounds, six ounces, with fair skin, blond hair, and blue eyes—a "regular Irish leprechaun," Marian thought, closely resembling her father-in-law. When the delivery room doctors examined Chris, they discovered none of the usual Down syndrome symptoms, such as a transverse palmer crease (a line that runs across the middle of the palm), extra skin at the back of the neck, or hypotonia, a general lack of muscle tone. They pronounced Chris a normal, healthy baby, and later, when Frank and the girls joined Marian in her hospital room, they were filled with delight.

Marian's pregnancy had been a surprise. After the birth of J. R. 12 years before, when Frank and Marian tried to have another child with no success, Marian had consulted her gynecologist. But in the early

Frank and Marian Burke depart for their honeymoon after their wedding in 1948.

1950s, little was known about infertility, so the doctor told her to be content with the three children she and Frank already had.

Then one day in 1965, Ellen came home from school to find her mother asleep on the couch. Ellen was astounded because her mother never took naps. When Marian woke, she and Ellen speculated that she probably had the flu, or a cold, but to Marian there was something familiar about her drowsiness and she wondered if she might be pregnant. That night she mentioned to Frank that she had fallen asleep after lunch and said that the last time she remembered doing that was when she was pregnant with J. R.

Frank laughed and said that if she were pregnant, he would buy her a mink coat.

A week later when Marian felt nauseous one morning, she recognized the early-pregnancy symptoms of morning sickness and made an appointment with her doctor. Marian had been right; she and Frank were going to have a baby. The children were thrilled about the prospective birth. Ellen was slightly embarrassed at having a pregnant mother because no one else in her high school class did, but as Marian's due date grew closer, the children became more and more excited. At Anne's graduation from grammar school, she was proud to have a happy, glowing, pregnant mother.

The family summered in Massapequa, Long Island, while Frank commuted from New York where he was a lieutenant in the police force and an instructor at the police academy. On August 25, Marian visited her doctor, who said that the baby would be arriving soon. That night she awoke with labor pains.

Frank rushed her 40 miles to St. Vincent's Hospital in Manhattan, where she used natural childbirth. (At that time natural childbirth, which substitutes breathing and relaxation exercises for anesthesia, was not common, although Marian had used the method with her other three children.) Christopher Joseph Burke was born on Thursday, August 26, after six hours of labor.

Later, after Frank and the girls had left the hospital, Marian fell asleep. She could not have been asleep more than a few minutes when the family pediatrician roused her to ask if she had seen the baby. Marian replied that of course she had seen him and he was beautiful. The doctor asked if she had noticed anything wrong with him.

Marian said that she had noticed two odd-looking white moles, but the doctor said that the moles were unimportant; instead, she asked if Marian had noticed anything odd about Chris's eyes. Marian had only observed that his eyes were bright blue like her father-in-law's.

"They're slanted," the pediatrician said. "The nurses noticed it first. The baby is a mongoloid."

The nurses in the infant nursery had noticed something that the delivery room doctors had missed. Chris's eyes were slanted upward at the outside, an indicator of Down syndrome called an *oblique* (slanted) *palpebral* (having to do with the eyelid) *fissure* (opening). The reason that the delivery room doctors had not noticed the symptom was that it was not severe in Chris.

The only way to determine with certainty whether Chris had Down syndrome was to take a blood test. He was found to have three 21st chromosomes, instead of the usual two. One out of every 800 to 1,000 infants has this condition. When a baby is conceived, the father's sperm fertilizes the mother's egg, producing a single cell with 23 chromosomes from the father and 23 from the mother, paired up like partners at a dance. In babies with Down syndrome, like Chris, there are three 21st chromosomes, instead of two, for reasons that researchers do not yet understand. Many doctors used to believe that the majority of Down syndrome babies were born to older mothers whose eggs had begun to change with age. (A female infant is born with all her eggs already formed in her ovaries; she never makes any additional ones.) The odds of having a baby with Down syndrome are slightly higher for older mothers. However, 80 percent of children born with Down syndrome are born to mothers under the age of 35.

Chris, like most people with Down syndrome, has an extra 21st chromosome in every cell in his body. But there is another type of Down syndrome, called mosaic pattern, in which only some cells have an extra chromosome. People with mosaic pattern Down syndrome tend to have less severe disabilities than those with the full syndrome, and some have above-average intelligence.

In the hospital the pediatrician was brusque with Marian. She told her to put Chris in an institution and said he would probably never walk or talk. When Marian called

John Langdon Down, an English doctor, was the first person to describe Down syndrome (which he called mongolism) in 1866. Down believed that if people with the syndrome were given the best education possible, they could achieve much more than was expected of them at the time. Unfortunately, this approach did not become the norm until a century later.

Frank at work, she was crying so hard he could barely understand her words.

The next few days, as his parents struggled to undertand Chris's condition, it seemed as if the Burkes were living in a nightmare. Frank was not familiar with the symptoms of "mongolism." Marian remembered a boy with Down syndrome who lived on the same street as she did when she was a child, and she knew two children with Down syndrome in Stuyvesant Town, the development where they were living at that time, but she had no facts about the syndrome. Few people did at that time. In recommending to the Burkes that they institutionalize Chris, their pediatrician was giving them standard medical advice.

Frank and Marian never wavered. "We had no decision to make," Frank said. "We were taking the baby home."

Ironically, the first person to identify Down syndrome, John Langdon Down, an English doctor who wrote a treatise on mental retardation in 1866, was optimistic about how much children with the syndrome could learn. He had observed that judicious treatment and careful training would reap rewards beyond what anyone could imagine, and he recommended that children with the syndrome be given the best education possible.

Unfortunately, the positive part of Down's findings was forgotten and the negative part remembered. Down reasoned that because people with Down syndrome have flat faces, short builds, and slanted eyes, they must somehow be related to the residents of Mongolia. From this he concluded that these "mongolians" were genetic throwbacks, belonging to a lower form of development than Englishmen such as himself. Down was using his cousin Charles Darwin's theory of evolution to hypothesize that some races are more highly evolved than others. (All such attempts to justify attitudes of racial superiority have since been completely discredited.)

In the years following Down's research and discovery, a few pioneering institutions gave care and schooling to children with Down syndrome, but most refused to give them life-saving medical care because it was thought that children with such a condition were better off dead. Children with Down syndrome were habitually strapped

A lithograph shows a person with a mental illness being kept in a cage in London in 1889. Treatment of the disabled has varied widely throughout history, ranging from reverence to loathing. In 1965, when Chris was born, a pediatrician advised the Burkes to put Chris in an institution and "forget you ever had him."

in high chairs and confined to cribs, which meant that they rarely learned to walk. In addition, they seldom learned to talk because their custodians did not speak to them enough. When the Burkes' pediatrician said that most children with Down syndrome could neither walk nor talk, she was describing the effects of institutionalization, not of the syndrome.

In the 1940s, 60 percent of children with Down syndrome died before their first birthday. (Today, average life expectancy for people with the syndrome is 55 years.) In the 1940s and 1950s, some states passed laws forcing parents to institutionalize children with the syndrome because it was believed that they would grow up to be violent and that, if they were kept at home, they would harm the development of their siblings. A theologian, Joseph Fletcher, even suggested in a 1968 article in the *Atlantic Monthly* that children with Down syndrome should be put to death at birth to save society the trauma of caring for them.

Such attitudes were all too prevalent at the time of Chris's birth in the 1960s, even among the medical profession. "They always acted as if I shouldn't want him," Marian remembers. The Burkes were overwhelmed by frustration. When Marian wanted Chris brought to her room so that she could cuddle him, nurses said he was undergoing tests, or gave some other excuse. The message that everyone seemed to be sending to the Burkes was that they should put Chris in a residential facility and forget about him.

If they had institutionalized Chris, he would have been placed in Willowbrook State School on Staten Island, a bleak complex sprawling across hundreds of acres, which served to store thousands of handicapped and mentally retarded people. In 1972, a TV report by ABC journalist Geraldo Rivera and others brought Willowbrook to public attention, exposing its filth and neglect. The scandal led to the closing of Willowbrook and other institutions like it all over the country and to the opening of small, community-based group homes where people with handicapping conditions could care for their own needs in a supervised setting.

But this was not to happen for another seven years. At St. Vincent's Hospital only two people encouraged the Burkes to keep Chris and care for him themselves. One was an intern who recommended that they bring him back later for more tests. The other person was a Catholic nun who told them to take Chris home and love him as he was.

Marian was released from the hospital a few days before Chris, who had to be kept for additional testing. As Marian was leaving, a nurse handed her a form to sign. When she asked what it was, the nurse explained that it was a guarantee that she would come back for her baby—the staff at St. Vincent's Hospital seemed to be worried that she might abandon Chris.

Marian was so upset and angry that she went home and scrubbed the entire apartment. Finally, a few days later, the Burkes were relieved to be able to bring Chris home. At first, they did not tell anyone that he had Down syndrome, explaining his extended stay at the hospital by saying that he had mild heart problems. Ellen, Anne, and J. R. noticed nothing unusual about Chris and enjoyed playing with him.

But every so often Frank and Marian would look at each other and their eyes would fill with tears. There were so many unknowns. He was a handsome baby now, but what would he look like when he was older? How much would he be able to learn? Would his presence be harmful to the other children? How would the other children react when they found out?

Ellen, Anne, and J. R., on the other hand, were bemused because their parents were not acting like themselves. For the first time in their memory, Marian and Frank had become anxious parents. Before Chris's birth, Frank and Marian had had an active social life, but since his birth they had been staying home every night. Marian seemed afraid to leave Chris for more than a few minutes at a time.

When Chris was a month and a half old, Frank dragged Marian to the New York World's Fair while Ellen baby-sat for Chris. Marian called every half hour to see how Chris was doing, making Ellen wonder why she was so concerned.

Anne was the first to guess the reason for her parents' anxiety. The Burke children had a friend with Down syndrome, an eight-year-old named Timmy who was part of a large family in Stuyvesant Town. Timmy's brothers and sisters included him in all their activities and took him everywhere, but it was obvious that Timmy was different. Anne looked at Chris one day and said she was not sure why, but Chris looked like Timmy. Her older sister, Ellen, said she was being silly, and the matter was dropped.

When Chris was nine months old, a friend of Ellen's pointed out that there was something odd about Chris's eyes, saying that they slanted upward. Ellen said it was nothing, but later in the day, after the friend had gone home and Marian and Ellen were alone in the kitchen, Marian said that Chris had mongolism. Ellen responded casually, "Oh, that's why you two are so worried over him."

Marian, encouraged by Ellen's mild reaction, told Anne and J. R. about Chris's condition. Anne was upset because she had seen adults with Down syndrome who had dull expressions and were overweight, and she was afraid that Chris would grow up to be like them. But at the moment Chris was a handsome, lively baby, and it was hard for her to imagine that he would ever become slow and obese. J. R., who was 12, refused to believe that there was

During a family vacation at Montauk, Long Island, Chris's sister Ellen shares a laugh with Chris, who was then one year old.

anything at all wrong with Chris. He told his parents that they did not know what they were talking about.

For Frank and Marian it was a great relief that the secret was finally out. At last, they could begin to relax and enjoy Chris. They were glad, though, that they had kept his condition secret for nine months because it had given the other children time to see Chris's strengths: his liveliness, curiosity, and warmth.

Chris cools off in a wash basin on a hot day in 1966.

3

A Ham Is Born

CHRIS WAS TREATED like a first child by Frank and Marian. Every time he did something new or wore a new outfit, they grabbed a camera, took a photograph, and hung it up. The walls became so covered with pictures of Chris that Ellen commented that the apartment had turned into a shrine to St. Christopher.

Chris's brothers and sisters seemed to take just as much delight in the new baby as his parents did. Marian was pleased to discover that "the fact that Chris had Down syndrome meant nothing to them. I told them that we all needed to work together with him. From that time on, it was as if he had five parents, not just two." In her opinion, having Chris around was good for the whole family. "It was marvelous to see the cohesiveness that resulted from us working together with him. The other children always took pride in Chris. They never hid him or were ashamed of him."

At two months of age Chris rolled over, much to the surprise of his pediatrician, who told Marian that it was probably an accident. When the time came for Chris to crawl, Marian put him on the floor and said to the children, "Let's show him what to do." For months the Burkes demonstrated proper crawling technique, until one day they found Chris crawling after them, gurgling with delight. (Today children with Down syndrome are taken out of their cribs and encouraged to crawl as soon as possible. Researchers have discovered that the exploration that goes with crawling is essential to cognitive development.)

Anne positioned Chris in front of a mirror, touching his eyes, ears, nose, and mouth, naming each feature and asking him to repeat the words after her. (This method has become a standard teaching device in early intervention programs.) J. R. took charge of Chris's athletic develop-

Twenty-month-old Justin Cowan crawls through a piece of exercise equipment designed especially for children with Down syndrome. Recent research has shown that with the proper stimulation and exercise, children with Down syndrome can achieve far more than was previously considered possible.

ment, showing him how to throw and catch as soon as he could hold a ball. (Today, programs for children with Down syndrome include exercise to correct their hypotonia, or poor muscle development.) Each morning Chris, who shared a bedroom with J. R., scrambled out of his crib and leapt onto J. R.'s bed to wake him. This practice did not bother J. R.—except when Chris's diapers needed to be changed.

To the delight of his family and the surprise of his pediatrician, Chris began to talk at 18 months and to walk at 2 years. Then one day Marian discovered that, despite all her efforts to help him, she might have inadvertently been holding Chris back. While on a brief vacation, Marian and Frank left Chris home with Ellen. To Marian's amazement, when they returned home, Chris was able to feed himself with a spoon. When she asked Ellen how she had taught him such a complex skill so quickly, Ellen shrugged and said that she had assumed that Chris could already feed himself, so she had put his spoon next to his plate and he had used it. Marian realized that Chris had probably been ready to feed himself all along.

Another discovery came while Marian was talking on the phone one day. In the next room Chris started yowling, amazing Marian, who had been wondering whether there was something wrong with his vocal cords because he never cried loudly. She realized that she had never given him a chance to cry; she had always run to comfort him at the least sign of distress. Marian was so thrilled by her discovery that she phoned Frank at the police academy. The woman who answered the phone assumed from Marian's excitement that there must be some kind of emergency, so she had Frank called out of class. Frank rushed to the phone to discover that Marian was calling to tell him that—at last!—Chris was screeching.

If Marian tended to be overprotective of Chris at first, the children wanted to push him ahead as quickly as possible. They drilled him with flash cards bearing letters, numbers, and simple words. When they were at the beach in the summer, they traced letters in the sand for Chris.

As Chris learned from Ellen, Anne, and J. R., they also learned from him. Anne, just entering high school, was suddenly in an environment where illegal drugs were easy to obtain. Watching Chris try so hard and seeing him struggle with skills that other children take for granted, she came to appreciate what she had, and she realized that it would be foolish of her to throw her own life away by falling into a world of drugs. The children also learned to be strong from watching their parents deal with Chris's limitations.

A Muppet judge presides over a pet show for an episode of "Sesame Street." The pioneering public television series became one of the first to feature an actor with Down syndrome when Jason Kingsley appeared on the show in the 1970s.

Frank and Marian were accustomed to dealing with adversity. Frank had been a prisoner of war in Germany during World War II; Marian's mother had died unexpectedly when Marian was only 28; and Anne had a bout with polio when she was a child. Over the years, Frank and Marian had developed a strategy for dealing with misfortune. On the anniversary of the day that Frank's plane was shot down over Germany, for example, Marian cooked him an elaborate dinner full of all the foods he had missed the most while starving in a P.O.W. camp. "If anything didn't go the way we wanted," said Marian, "the first chance we had, we would go out and celebrate. It was our way of saying, 'We'll work it out. We'll make the best of it.'" They dealt with Chris's disability the same way. "We tried to get up and get on with life, not let this burden us," Frank said. "The kids saw how we reacted to that."

There were some aspects of Down syndrome, however, that the Burkes could not deal with alone. One of the symptoms of the syndrome is abnormal ear development, which causes children to have difficulty hearing word endings, such as *ing* and *ed.* Children with Down syndrome are also confused by differences in pronunciation. A Southern accent, for instance, can baffle a child who has grown up in New York. Furthermore, the same word can be pronounced differently by the same person, who may, for example, say, "Nooooooo?" to express doubt and, "No!" to express anger. Chris needed speech therapy to develop his language comprehension. He also needed help with his pronunciation because he had a narrow mouth and limited muscle development in his tongue, and he tended to stutter when he was excited.

Unfortunately, when it came to finding a qualified speech therapist who was willing to work with a preschool child with Down syndrome, Marian discovered that her choices were few. She finally located one on 115th Street, but the bus trip from their home was long and exhausting.

When Chris was three years old, his parents entered him in weekly classes for special children. Chris amazed his teachers with his skill in reading flash cards. They did not know that he was a graduate of the Burke tutoring school. At home Chris watched the new television program "Sesame Street," singing and dancing along with the Muppets, and yelling, "This program is brought to you by the letter J." One night he grabbed a banana and talked into it as though it were a phone, pretending to be Oscar the Grouch.

The Burkes tried to learn everything they could about Down syndrome. Marian checked the New York Public Library's holdings, but all she could find were medical textbooks that were difficult to understand. (Today, there are books and videotapes about Down syndrome for people with the syndrome and for their families. See Further Reading, page 108.) Anne wrote to former vice-president Hubert Humphrey because she had heard that his granddaughter had Down syndrome. Humphrey responded to her in detail, describing what he had learned and including a list of family support groups in New York City.

Marian, eager to meet other parents in a similar situation, visited one of the groups, but it turned out to be a discouraging experience. Members complained about how hard it was to be a parent of a child with Down syndrome. Marian, who felt that Chris was a delight, decided that such support groups were not for her.

Seeking out friends for Chris, Marian took him to a playground near their apartment in Stuyvesant Town, but many mothers pulled their children away, as if Chris might hurt them. (Some people believed that Down syndrome children were violent, while others believed that they were happy and angelic. In fact, people with the syndrome have the same range of emotions as everyone else.) In the summer of 1968, while Chris was playing on the beach at Massapequa near the Burke summer home, he walked over to a girl who was his own age, but her mother rushed over, pulling her away. "He's not contagious," Ellen said, and led him to another part of the beach.

The Burkes realized that they had to find a preschool program where Chris could make friends. Then Frank discovered the Kennedy Child Study Center, which was located on the same street as the 19th Precinct building where he worked. Founded in honor of President John F. Kennedy's mentally retarded sister, Rosemary, the center was one of the first to combine numerous disciplines—pediatrics, neurology, psychology, education—to foster the development of retarded children.

Unfortunately, Sister Arthur Marie, the head of the center, had to tell Frank that Chris was too young for their program. (Today, the Kennedy Child Study Center begins to work with children within weeks of birth, but in the late 1960s Catholic Charities, a national organization that supported the center, could not justify spending money on such an experimental practice.)

By the time Chris was four years old, the center had a play group that he was able to attend twice a week. At last, while he was playing, Marian had the opportunity to talk to experts and ask questions. For the first time she received solid, supportive advice about raising Chris, and, in the context of the center, she could see that he was doing well. Many of the other children were withdrawn. Chris, on the other hand, was friendly and full of fun.

At five he was one of the youngest students ever to attend the Kennedy Child Study Center full-time. His academic level was just above average for a child with Down syndrome. (Most people with the syndrome have an I.Q. of under 70 and are mildly or moderately retarded.) But he was unusually self-sufficient for his age. Unlike many of the other children, he had no problem separating from his mother.

One of Chris's most striking characteristics was his warmth. When visitors arrived in the classroom, as they often did, other children tended to avoid them, but Chris was an instant greeter, showing guests around the classroom as if it belonged to him. He was equally affectionate toward the other children. For example, when he encouraged an autistic girl to participate in a game, she did not respond, but Chris kept coaxing her until one day, to the amazement of the teachers, she joined the group.

The curriculum of the play group was carefully planned to foster the physical, social, and intellectual development

Chris's sister Anne takes him for a bicycle ride in 1971.

of Chris and the other children. Finger painting improved their muscle control and sense of touch. Musical chairs and circle games strengthened muscle tone. Chris and the other children played with oversize letters to learn to spell their names. One morning at breakfast Chris amazed his family by pointing to the letters on a Cheerios cereal box and picking out the letters of his name.

Dressing up and playing make-believe were his favorite activities. Sometimes children in the play group put on plays. In later years Chris did not remember much of his time at the Kennedy Center, partly because people with Down syndrome tend to have poor long-term memories, but he remembered the first play he appeared in—*The Emperor's New Clothes.* His role was not a big one, consisting of only two lines: "Hark, who goes there?" and "Ha, ha, ha, what a joke." But years later he could still remember his lines and the applause he received. "It was a lot of fun," Chris recalled. "That was when I decided I wanted to be an actor, when I was five years old."

"He's always been a big ham," a friend of the Burkes', Fran Slattery, remembered:

> He would perform at the drop of a hat. He has a good sense of rhythm, and kept up with all the newest music. We were astounded by his memory. He could tell you all these things about movies and television. And he always thought to ask me about my children, how they were doing. My mother got the biggest kick out of him. She'd say, "You're telling me this boy's retarded?" She didn't believe it at all. But he was surrounded by a wonderful, loving family. He was always a secure, confident, well-rounded person with a great deal of sensitivity to others.

At home he pored over Ellen's, Anne's, and J. R.'s portfolios from the days when they appeared in TV and magazine ads. Anne, with her red hair and freckles, had been the most popular of the three, starring in a TV commercial that ran for years and posing for a bubble gum ad that appeared every Halloween for almost 20 years.

J. R. had nearly become a star, having been a runner-up for a leading role in the hit TV series "Flipper."

The scrapbooks seemed to convince Chris that he could be a star as well. But when he told Marian that someday he was going to be on television, she felt sad. Although it was true that Chris was the same age that J. R., Anne, and Ellen were when they started their careers, it did not seem likely that he would ever have one. Not wanting to set Chris up for disappointment, Marian said that she doubted there would be parts for him. Chris replied, "Well, you never know."

Chris loved to entertain at family parties. His favorite stage was the staircase at his cousin Pat Egan's house. After dinner he would hurry into the living room to push

At age seven, Chris receives congratulations from his teacher on graduation day at the Kennedy Child Study Center.

chairs and couches into viewing position and then, when everyone was seated, he stood on the staircase singing, lip-synching to a record, or telling jokes. His family could not always understand him, but they laughed and clapped anyway. The night before his First Communion, the family came into Pat Egan's living room and found that Chris had prepared a table with a cloth and candles for a make-believe mass. Chris played the role of priest, while J. R. and his cousin were altar boys. The family was amazed to discover that Chris knew the ritual by heart.

Around 1970, experts stopped calling Chris's condition "mongolism," referring to it instead as Down's syndrome. The name was later changed to Down syndrome because Down did not personally have the syndrome; he simply described it. Marian remembered, "We were so thrilled to have a new word for it. It sounded so much better." Chris, however, did not like the negative sound of Down syndrome and preferred to use his own phrase, Up syndrome.

Chris and his friend Matthew (left) enjoy a visit from Chris's brother-in-law Jack (right) at the Cardinal Cushing School in Hanover, Massachusetts.

4

A Pine Tree in His Lungs

WHEN SEVEN-YEAR-OLD CHRIS graduated from the Kennedy Child Study Center, the Burkes had to find a new school for him. At that time, New York City public schools did not practice mainstreaming, a system in which children with handicaps are placed in regular school classes. (Today, children with Down syndrome are almost always mainstreamed.) Frank and Marian visited special education classes in several New York City public schools and were not impressed by what they saw. Classes seemed more like play groups. "It was strictly adequate," Frank recalled. "We wanted more than adequate for all of our children, and especially for Chris."

When Chris was still a baby, the Burkes had seen a TV special called "The Long Childhood of Timmy." The star of the special was their neighbor Timmy from Stuyvesant Town, and the program showed him leaving home for St. Coletta's School (later renamed Cardinal Cushing

School and Training Center) in Hanover, Massachusetts. The school seemed like a warm, comfortable place with private dorm rooms and a wide range of stimulating activities. Frank and Marian believed that Chris would find it challenging.

They had taken Chris to visit the school every year since he was two years old, and after his graduation from the Kennedy Center they felt he was ready to attend the school in Massachusetts. (Today, with mainstreaming, children with Down syndrome are less likely to go to boarding schools.) As the time came for Chris to leave, Marian became more and more agitated. Cardinal Cushing School was a four-hour drive from New York City, and Chris was only eight years old. Marian could not help wondering whether she and Frank were doing the right thing. Whenever she looked at Chris, her eyes filled with tears, but Frank assured her that they were doing what was best for Chris.

As they drove Chris to Cardinal Cushing School for a two-week visit, Frank reminded Marian that the school would help Chris in ways they could not. Chris would make new friends and acquire new skills; he would get as much speech therapy as he needed. At the school the Burkes watched Chris meet and play with other children until a nun suggested that it was time for them to leave. Marian went to Chris, knelt down and hugged him. Frank was about to kneel to hug him when Chris stretched himself as tall as he could and said, "Dad, big boys don't hug. They shake hands."

Frank shook Chris's hand, left the room with Marian, and fell apart. They drove around for two hours while Frank cried and tried to pull himself together. Finally, they realized they were too tired to return to New York and checked into a hotel.

Chris, on the other hand, was delighted by Cardinal Cushing School. There were so many people to meet, so many questions to ask. Janitors, cooks, visitors—everyone

Chris, at around age 10, vacations with his family in Cape Cod, Massachusetts. His busy lifestyle and the many activities he enjoyed with his family helped him overcome hypotonia, or poor muscle tone, a common side effect of Down syndrome.

fascinated him. An initial two-week trial visit stretched into a permanent stay. By the end of the semester Chris was one of the best-known children at the school.

The staff soon learned that Chris was never where they expected him to be. Sometimes he hid in a storage area, other times behind furniture. Frequently he went exploring around the school grounds. The staff did not worry, however, because it soon became apparent that Chris knew how to take care of himself.

Academically, Chris was an average student, but socially he was far above average. Teachers knew they could rely on him to take care of younger children or newcomers who felt shy. He loved to run errands for the staff and he was capable of being serious when it was important that he behave responsibly. As an altar boy, he was solemn and well prepared, offering special prayers for his family, his teachers, and people he had heard about who were in distress.

With his freckles, fair skin, and thick blond hair, he was one of the most handsome children at the school, and he was also a natty dresser, wearing polo shirts, khakis, and, for special occasions, a jacket and tie or a suit. He even carried his papers in an attaché case and earned the nickname the Little Prep. "He could have easily won best-dressed award at school," remembered Vicky Anderson, a teacher at Cardinal Cushing.

He did not find it difficult to adjust to being in a boarding school. Other children became homesick or had difficulty adapting to dorm life, but Chris fit in immediately. He socialized so much that he was often late to class. Once he was so late that he picked flowers for his teacher and dramatically presented them to her before she could scold him for his tardiness.

Once each month he and his neighbor Timmy flew home to New York for a visit. Chris would deplane carrying souvenir magazines, air sickness bags, or anything else portable, with a couple of stewardesses in tow.

After spending the weekend at home, Chris was never resentful about having to return to school, as many of the other children were. At show-and-tell he talked proudly about his family's trips and J. R.'s adventures in college.

Chris continued to grow academically. At nine he was reading at a second grade level, and in other subjects he was working close to grade level. What he enjoyed studying most, though, were plays. Some evenings he and his friends would retreat to a small room where they could make up skits and improvise costumes. Chris would assemble stage sets and write tickets, and then they would perform for the student body of 150 children.

The most unusual thing about Chris's love of drama was its persistence. Other students at Cardinal Cushing were equally adept at acting or improvising but did not stay

Marian Burke helps Chris celebrate his 10th birthday with his friends.

involved as long as Chris did. "Others would go through a phase of being interested," a nun recalled, "but he kept at it. Chris was an actor all along, and very good." He even acted in regular classes, pretending to be the Fonz from the TV sitcom "Happy Days" or imitating a rock star and playing an imaginary guitar. When Chris had to answer questions, he would drop his voice and talk in the deep, mellow tones of a radio announcer, to the delight of his classmates.

Cardinal Cushing School was a coeducational institution, and as Chris grew toward adolescence, girls began to interest him. He had a few casual friendships, and then, when he was 12, a more serious one. He would take his girlfriend to the movies and carry her books on the way to class.

In 1975, during Chris's second year at Cardinal Cushing, Congress passed Public Law 194–42, which declared that all students were entitled to receive an education in the least restrictive environment. This meant that children with special needs had to be mainstreamed whenever possible. Because of the new law, many of the children who were at Cardinal Cushing lost their government financial aid and transferred to public schools. (The Burkes had tried to obtain government funding for Chris's education, but they had failed because the family earned enough money to pay for his tuition on their own.) Cardinal Cushing's student body began to change after the enactment of the law. Fewer of the students were mentally retarded and more of them had behavioral problems, like outbursts of aggression or an inability to form relationships. Many of the new students had been shunted from one foster care home to another, and many had suffered from abuse or neglect.

One of the new students, a boy who had been abandoned at birth, took a special dislike to Chris. The boy was not retarded but had severe learning disabilities and was desperate for attention. He found Chris's popularity infuriating.

One weekend in March, when the students had just left the dining hall, the new boy ran over to Chris and said, "Open your mouth and close your eyes and I'll give you a big surprise." When Chris played along with the game and opened his mouth, the boy stuffed it full of pine needles. Choking and gasping, Chris tried to cough out the needles, but inhaled some instead. The school's staff rushed him to the hospital for X rays, which were inconclusive.

When Chris returned to Cardinal Cushing School, he was frightened, talking about the incident in his classes and writing about it for the school paper. Chris told the boy who had stuffed his mouth with pine needles that he did not like what he had done, but then Chris offered to be friends. "It was something very touching to watch," said Vicky Anderson. "I wouldn't be able to do that. He really forgave him, and it helped the boy a lot."

There was no repeat of the incident, but for the rest of the year Chris was bothered by a racking, wheezing cough. He became less talkative in class, turning listless and lazy. That summer at Point Lookout, he was quiet, often sleeping on the sand instead of socializing as he usually had done. Marian took him to a number of doctors, but all of them said that children with Down syndrome are prone to a host of minor illnesses and that his condition was probably a respiratory infection that would clear up with time.

In the fall of 1975, still weak, Chris went back to Cardinal Cushing School. One weekend Frank and Marian met him at the New York airport to drive to Washington, D.C., to see Ellen, but by the time they got to Virginia he was coughing blood. Frank and Marian took him to a hospital but once again doctors said that it was normal for people with Down syndrome to have respiratory infections. In Washington the next day, Marian took him to another doctor who thought there might be a foreign object in Chris's lungs and wanted to operate, but Marian decided to return to the family's regular pediatrician in New York. The pediatrician took X rays, which failed to show any obstructions. The doctor told Marian that children like Chris get pneumonia often; Marian replied that Chris had never had pneumonia before.

At Cardinal Cushing, even though the staff gave Chris treatments prescribed by his doctor, his coughing spells became worse. Chris was rushed to the hospital three times, and each time, using a bronchoscope (a lighted tube that is pushed down the throat), doctors extracted pine needles from his lungs. Every time they performed the procedure, they believed they had removed the last of the needles. Marian, who had become skeptical by now, asked the hospital to make an exploratory operation, but the doctors believed that surgery would be too dangerous for Chris.

When Chris returned home for summer vacation in 1976, he seemed to be doing better until a noodle got caught in his throat at a restaurant and he started to cough up blood. Deciding to listen to her own instincts, Marian arranged an operation for him in Boston. Eighteen months

Chris proudly displays a fish he caught while on vacation in Cape Cod.

after his classmate gave him a mouthful of pine needles, Chris prepared to go into surgery.

J. R., having graduated from college, was traveling around the world, but when he heard that Chris was going into surgery, he cut his trip short, arriving just in time to greet Chris as he was wheeled out of the operating room. The doctors had discovered that a pine seed had sprouted in the warm, moist environment of Chris's lungs. They had removed a one-inch pine tree.

Chris enjoys his first ocean cruise at age 12 with his parents. Chris was exceptionally well traveled; he accompanied his parents to Poland and Colombia, to visit his sister Ellen, and vacationed in Florida, Bermuda, the Bahamas, and Nashville, Tennessee.

5

Warner Brothers Calling

THE CARDINAL CUSHING SCHOOL staff told the Burkes that they should find another school for Chris because the student body had changed so much he no longer belonged there. Frank and Marian agreed that the transfer was necessary, and in any case, the cost of having Chris commute from Boston to New York once a month, and the complications of meeting airplanes and making connections, had become too much for them. They wanted to find a school closer to home.

J. R. and Chris had always had a close relationship. When Chris was two years old, the family had left him with friends while they went on a brief vacation. Returning home, the Burke children argued about whom Chris would hug first. Anne insisted he would go straight for her. J. R. said he would come to him. Marian did not say anything but she was sure that Chris would greet her first. When Chris saw his family, he let out a shout of joy and ran right into J. R.'s arms.

In 1978, J. R. was living in Philadelphia and commencing a career in insurance and finance. He began searching for a school in the area that would provide a caring and challenging environment for Chris. In nearby Springfield, he found the Don Guanella school, which had been established by an order of Italian priests in 1960 to educate mentally retarded people. It had an enrollment of 130, smaller than Cardinal Cushing School, but it had more elaborate facilities with two miles of woods, an indoor swimming pool, a pond, a football field, and two basketball courts. At night students gathered for games, dancing, and skits, activities that the Burkes thought Chris was sure to like. The food served was authentic Italian cuisine because the kitchen staff had been taught to prepare the priests' favorite dishes.

The student residences at the Don Guanella school, shown here, are set amid comfortable grounds that include two miles of woods and a pond.

When Chris enrolled in the school, he was thrilled to be near J. R. Some nights J. R. visited Don Guanella to shoot a few baskets with Chris and his friends. Every other weekend Chris slept at J. R.'s house, usually bringing friends, and J. R. would take them to restaurants, movies, and basketball games. Soon Chris's friends were J. R.'s, and J. R.'s friends were Chris's. On the other weekends, Chris took the train to New York. He enjoyed these rides as much as he had enjoyed the airplane flights to Boston. Chris became friends with the New York City stationmaster. As soon as he reached the station, Chris made it a game to sneak off the train and hide in the stationmaster's office. The stationmaster would turn on the public address system and say, "Will Mr. and Mrs. Francis D. Burke please come to the stationmaster's office?" and then Frank, Marian, and Chris would hold their reunion with the stationmaster smiling on. "Every single time, we would get to the station before the train came in," Frank remembers, "and no matter how hard we tried, he always managed to slip away before we saw him. I still don't know how he did it."

At 13, Chris still looked like an adorable eight-year-old boy, but a year later he had begun to mature, growing thinner and almost a foot taller. His hair darkened, and he took to wearing it shoulder length, hippie-style. He began to listen to heavy metal music, which could be heard blaring continually from his tape deck. Chris was still polite and well behaved and treated his mother with deference, opening doors for her and seating her at the table, but he had the usual adolescent problems. "I had a lot of fun," he recalled later, "but I had growing pains, too. Sometimes it was rough."

To Chris, Don Guanella was not quite the ideal place it had seemed to his family. Chris was put in a huge dormitory room with 20 other boys. In the mornings, rock music blasted students out of bed, and Chris, who was a slow riser, often had trouble getting dressed. One day, after Chris visited his mother's aunt Sally in a nursing home, he asked if he could buy a white wig. Puzzled, his parents asked him why he wanted one. Chris replied that then he could move into the nursing home and be Aunt Sally's roommate. To him, at that moment, the nursing home seemed like a place of relative freedom and privacy.

Chris's biggest difficulty at Don Guanella was the school's point system. Students earned privileges through doing chores, being on time, and being neat, but promptness and neatness had never been Chris's strengths, and he lost points for not making his bed. He lost more points for playing his heavy metal music too loud. "I didn't know anything about a point system," Chris recalled. "I didn't like it because they treated me like I was in the army. They were always telling me to do this or that. If I got higher points, I could stay up late. If I got lower points, I had to go to bed early, and I couldn't go on field trips." But Chris was never in any serious trouble. "He was a good kid," remembered the priest who supervised his residence hall. "He didn't bother anyone."

The student body at Don Guanella had changed, however, just as it had at Cardinal Cushing School. Don Guanella had been founded to educate retarded children, but because of Public Law 194–42, many had switched to state-funded public schools. When Chris arrived at Don Guanella, half the students attending the school had emotional or behavioral problems. Many of them came from abusive homes or detention facilities. Many did not like being placed with retarded students and sometimes beat them up and made fun of them.

Chris himself was never physically injured because he was so gentle and sincere that the other students would not hit him. Instead, they made fun of him or mimicked his stuttering. "Some of my friends would make fun of me and tease me," Chris recalled. "I don't really think it's fair, calling names at other people."

At first Chris tried too hard to make friends, and others took advantage of him. "This one boy had a rule that I wasn't allowed to pass his part of the hallway," Chris recalled. "I couldn't even go visit my friends. He got me so wound up. I got in trouble and I didn't even do anything to him." Once, a boy killed two hamsters and tried to frame Chris by putting the hamsters' bodies in a garbage can and pouring Chris's vitamin tablets on top to make it look like Chris had done it. "He killed these innocent little animals," Chris remembered. "I wanted to beat him up."

Chris rarely complained to his parents, so they thought that compared to Cardinal Cushing, Don Guanella was peaceful and orderly. "We didn't realize that he went from the frying pan into the fire," Marian said later. Soon, though, Chris found ways of coping with his tormentors. Staff members helped him see that trying too hard to ingratiate himself only made his problems worse. He learned to rely on his strengths, such as his gift for performing. When break-dancing became popular, he learned how to whirl and roll with the best of them. When other students talked about sports, he was able to show off his sports knowledge because he, J. R., and Frank had been Mets and Giants fans for years. When other students made fun of him, he told them how he felt and what they had done to make him feel that way. "You can't find that many adults who can do that," one of his counselors said.

Chris thrived academically, and within a few years he moved from a class with students his own age to a class with older children. For a person with Down syndrome this was a highly unusual occurrence. What excited him the most, however, was that the school encouraged him to follow through on his plan to make his own movie. When he was 14, Chris started writing a screenplay based on the Anne Murray song, "Just Falling in Love Again." He spent most of the year working on the plot and dialogue, and then in the spring, with a finished script in hand, he got classmates to act in it. The story is about two soldiers who long to return home to their wives, and a performance was filmed on videotape.

Chris receives a medal at the Special Olympics at age 15. Exercise is especially important for people with Down syndrome. Many of the physical problems caused by the syndrome can be alleviated by doing the proper exercises.

Chris also had daily speech therapy at Don Guanella. Like many people with Down syndrome, he had trouble enunciating certain sounds, such as *r, k, dr,* and *str.* He occasionally dropped word endings and sometimes left out short words like *a* and *the.* Part of his problem was that at times he talked so fast that his words became jumbled. His therapist taught him to tap his fingers in a steady rhythm to keep his language flowing evenly. In conversation, Chris sometimes had difficulty sticking to a single subject, and his speech therapist would have to bring him back to his original topic. But often the therapist was amazed at

Chris's broad knowledge of the world. For example, one day, when the therapist said he was excited about visiting friends in San Francisco, Chris mentioned that he and his family were about to leave for Poland to visit his sister Ellen, whose husband was in the foreign service.

At 16, Chris discovered country music. Singers who performed at the Grand Ole Opry, such as Randy Travis, became his favorites. Chris dreamed of going to Nashville, Tennessee, and begged his parents to plan a vacation there. They finally gave in to his prodding, and when the three

When he reached his midteens, Chris fell in love with country music; one of his favorite singers was Randy Travis, shown here. Chris explained, "I like country music because it tells a story. I like it because they sing their hearts out. And it's honest."

of them arrived in Nashville, Frank and Marian were surprised to discover that they were as fascinated by the origins of country music as Chris was.

Chris still harbored dreams of entering show business himself, and he would frequently write to stars such as Donny and Marie Osmond, telling them about his plans and saying he hoped to meet them someday. When he was 17, Chris got a temporary job stuffing envelopes for the company where his mother worked. He saved his earnings and bought a videocassette recorder so that he could study his favorite movies in earnest. He became adept at programming his VCR and would replay programs until he memorized all the lines.

Two years later, in 1985, Chris saw Jason Kingsley, the young actor with Down syndrome, on the TV show "The Fall Guy" and became even more convinced that he could make it as an actor. From corresponding with Jason's mother, Emily Kingsley, Chris learned that Jason had been a regular on "Sesame Street" and the talk show circuit. Chris told friends and teachers at Don Guanella that he was going to be a star like his new friend Jason Kingsley, but no one believed him. The Mother Superior of Don Guanella recalled, "He always said, 'When I'm big, I want to be a movie star.' I would tell him, 'That's nice,' and encourage him. To myself, I was laughing. I never thought he could go that far." But one of his teachers, Robert Neely, did see Chris's talent and enrolled him in an acting workshop for disabled students. There, Chris learned about improvisation, characterization, and camera angles.

At graduation in 1986, Chris had neither job prospects nor practical plans. Though this situation did not upset him because he was sure that he was going to be a star, his family thought his plan was unrealistic. J. R. had brought a video camera to the graduation ceremony, but seeing Chris up on the stage in his cap and gown, and realizing that Chris had no reasonable plans for his future, J. R. became so agitated that he had to step outside to get control of himself. "It really hit home to me that now we were talking about the rest of his life," J. R. remembered. "He was sheltered and isolated a bit when he was in school. Now we were talking about real world stuff. He was going to have to go out and get a job."

Meanwhile, out on the West Coast, writer and producer Michael Braverman was writing a script for an ABC TV pilot called "Desperate," about a ship captain, shattered by failure, who is trying to put his life back together. As

Chris enjoys a helicopter ride while home for the weekend from the Don Guanella school in Springfield, Pennsylvania. Graduation from Don Guanella in 1986 left Chris facing an uncertain future.

written, the drama had only one character, a situation that rarely works on TV. "I needed a character who would act as the hero's conscience," Braverman recalled. "A sidekick of sorts. Someone who would always tell the truth."

When Braverman had been a writer for the television show "Magnum P.I.," Tom Selleck, the star, asked him to come up with an episode about the Special Olympics. Braverman had interviewed children with Down syndrome for the episode, which never aired. But he never forgot the experience, and now Braverman realized that the perfect character to play the captain's companion would be a young person with Down syndrome. Braverman called a Warner Brothers casting director and asked her to hold auditions. In December 1986, more than 50 young men with Down syndrome answered the casting call, including Jason Kingsley. When the director told Jason that he was too young for the role, Jason's mother suggested that Warner Brothers contact Chris Burke.

That night the casting director called the Burkes' residence and asked if Chris could come for an audition. Chris, of course, was overjoyed. After all his hard work, his dreams seemed to be coming true at last. The next day Marian brought Chris to the Warner Brothers office at New York City's Rockefeller Center and he auditioned for the part in competition with several other actors.

When Braverman received the videotape of Chris's audition, he knew he had found the right actor for the role. But the script was not ready to be shot. For two months Braverman wrote and polished dialogue while the Burkes wondered what had happened to the show. At first Chris's hopes were sky high, but as weeks passed, and then months, he became less optimistic. His parents, trying to ease the blow, reminded him that someone else might have gotten the part, or that ABC might have decided not to produce the pilot at all. (Of the 250 scripts that ABC receives each year from studios such as Warner Brothers, it usually asks for only about 30 pilots to be filmed.)

Then, on a Monday night in February 1987 the Burkes' phone rang. The Warner Brothers casting director wanted to know if Chris could be in Los Angeles by Wednesday. "You should have seen my mom's expression," Chris laughingly remembered. Marian, who so far had been calm and skeptical, put the phone to her shoulder and called, "Frank! Frank! Chris is going to Hollywood!"

In February 1987, Chris Burke's lifelong dream came true when he was invited to Hollywood, California, to audition for a part in a television show.

6

Life Is an Elevator

THE BURKES SCARCELY had time to tell their family and friends about Chris's good fortune before it was time for him to leave for California. Frank had retired from the New York City police force and was now a security executive at a bank. But as it happened, he was on vacation at the time, so he and Chris packed their bags and flew to Los Angeles.

At the Warner Brothers studio Chris read scenes from the script to Michael Braverman and Warner executives. "I wasn't nervous," Chris recalled. "They were very nice. I liked Michael right away." When the Warner executives agreed that Chris was right for the part, he was taken to ABC where he read the script again. Afterward he was asked to wait outside with his father. A few minutes later Braverman called Chris into the room to tell him that they had decided to give him the part. Chris let out a joyful whoop and went dancing down the hallway to where his father was waiting and gave him a big hug. This was the moment that he had been planning and preparing for his whole life. His hard work and faith in himself had paid off: Chris Burke was going to be on TV. What meant the most to Frank was that Chris had reached his goal by his own initiative. "We were all so elated over the fact that Chris had done this on his own."

On the flight back to New York, the Burkes' airline tickets were upgraded to first class, a sign of Chris's new status. Chris only had a few days to spend there before proceeding to Florida, where the pilot would be filmed. The next morning he went to P.S. 138, which was just a few blocks from the Burkes' apartment, and headed straight for Tom Roeder's classroom, where he was working as a volunteer. After he told Roeder and a few other friends about the audition and showed them the script, word of his success spread throughout the building. The staff of P.S. 138 remembered that one of Chris's goals had been to be an actor by the age of 23. He had beaten his target date by two years.

Frank decided to retire from his bank job two weeks early, so his co-workers threw him a hasty farewell party. The next day a limousine took Frank and Chris to the airport, where they boarded a plane to Florida, flying first class. In Key West another limousine met them and took them to a hotel suite that had a view of the Atlantic Ocean.

They visited the set. "It was all so new to us," said Frank. "We were even excited about seeing the director's chairs with the stars' names on the back." They were amazed to see that one sound stage had trash on the floor and cobwebs in the corners. Frank asked a crew member when they were going to clean it up. The crew member laughed and said that the dirt was part of the set and that it had taken them hours to get the cobwebs in place.

Chris and Frank had to learn how to behave on a set while shooting was in progress. They soon learned that they had to keep out of the way of the crew, avoid walking in front of the lights, and never wander into a scene. Chris was thrilled to find that John Savage was playing the lead role in the drama because Savage had appeared in some of Chris's favorite movies, including *Inside Moves, The Deer Hunter,* and *Hair.* But Chris quickly learned that he could not visit Savage's trailer any time he wished because Savage had lines to learn and scenes to study.

When Chris filled up on catered meals on the set, Frank cautioned him not to eat too much in order to save production expenses. Soon, though, Frank realized that there was plenty of food available and it did not matter how much they ate. "It was such a new life for us," said Frank. "We felt a little like royalty at first."

Braverman told the cast and crew that they would be working with an actor with Down syndrome but that they should treat Chris the way they would treat any actor.

Filming for Chris Burke's first appearance on a television program—the pilot for a proposed series, "Desperate"—took place in Key West, Florida. Here Chris and his mother enjoy a side trip to the nearby EPCOT Center at Disney World in Orlando.

There was no standby in case Burke could not handle the part. Sometimes Chris became tired and forgot his lines and sometimes his concentration faltered, but his fellow actors were amazed at the depth of his feelings and how genuine and sincere he appeared on film. "He has this acceptance of himself, and he is so accepting of others," said Meg Foster, one of the show's costars. "When you accept your limitations and you know what they are, you all of a sudden are boundless."

Once they got used to his limitations, his fellow actors found that Burke's strengths as an actor more than made up for his weaknesses. As Foster put it, "There's a joy and love of life and being in the moment which is an actor's goal. Chris doesn't have to work for that. He is the moment. He is the actor."

After 18 days in Key West, Chris flew to Los Angeles to shoot interior scenes. A week later he was back at P.S. 138. He showed his friends photographs of John Savage and Meg Foster and told them he was sure that ABC was going to turn the pilot into a series, but his friends were skeptical.

His doubting friends turned out to be correct. When ABC aired "Desperate" in April, viewers and critics agreed that although Burke's acting was excellent, the script was not effective overall. ABC decided not to expand the pilot into a TV series. When Michael Braverman phoned with the news, Frank and Marian were disappointed, but also slightly relieved that the family would not be uprooted. Chris felt sad, but he was not miserable because he was planning to pursue his work at P.S. 138 and take acting classes on the side. Eileen Himick, the coordinator of the Young Adult Institute, where Chris was taking acting classes, said, "When Chris came back, he was still the same old Chris. He wasn't coming in and bragging about it. Then when the pilot wasn't picked up, Chris didn't mope around. He wasn't angry. He was confident something else would come along. There was no change

"Desperate" was aired as a television movie in April 1987, but the show was not turned into a series. Still, Chris was thrilled to have had the chance to perform with John Savage (center) and Meg Foster, and his acting made a lasting impression on executives at ABC, setting the stage for future work with the network.

in that determination. It was as if he saw the path that none of us could see."

Mark Buchan, Burke's teacher at the institute, remembers that Chris "talked all the time about wanting to get on another pilot and have a television series. I thought he had delusions. I know thousands of actors who want to be in a television series. It never occurred to me that someone with Down syndrome could have their own show." Nevertheless, Buchan was impressed by Chris's dedication. "He had a good deal in common with actors I know who have had commercial success. . . . He worked on his career the same way those successful actors work on their careers. He was one of the most ambitious actors I have ever met."

Meanwhile, in Los Angeles, ABC executives had not forgotten Burke. They had been disappointed by the pilot, but they had been impressed by him. "Although ABC did not pick up that pilot, they loved Chris so much in it, they asked me if I could do something to develop a show that featured him," Braverman recalled. "I tried a bunch of things and determined that I couldn't do a series where he was the lead. He wouldn't be able to handle it." Instead, Braverman came up with the idea of doing a family show with Chris as part of an ensemble cast.

In New York the Burkes, knowing nothing of what was being planned, settled back into their normal life. As the excitement over "Desperate" diminished, Chris was offered a paying job at P.S. 138. The school district had ordered P.S. 138 to convert a freight elevator into a passenger elevator for the use of students and teachers, but because many of the children at P.S. 138 needed help getting in and out of elevators, it became apparent that an operator was needed. Pat Mulholland, an assistant principal and a friend of Chris's, went to the district office and said that she thought that it was deplorable that the entire district, which served handicapped children, did not employ a single handicapped person. She said she wanted to put Chris on the payroll as an elevator operator.

Hiring Chris was no simple matter because supervisors at the Board of Education were concerned about liability in case of accident. They were also dubious that Chris would be able to handle severely handicapped children. But Mulholland and the district coordinator drew up a detailed proposal and convinced the board that Chris could handle the job.

Chris started operating the elevator as a volunteer in January. Then on February 3, 1988, he became the first person with a mental disability to be hired by the district. He gained medical and dental insurance and civil service status. To Frank and Marian, Chris's position at the school was a lot better than one in show business. They were still wary of Chris pinning his hopes on acting, which more than likely would turn out to be a flash in the pan. But a full-time, paid position with medical and retirement benefits would fulfill their dream of Chris being independent, productive, and self-sufficient. And Chris was following a family tradition because during the depression Frank's father had been an elevator operator.

At first, Chris had trouble getting used to the demands of the job. During his first staff meetings he sometimes did not pay attention and went into the next room to watch a movie on videocassette, until Pat Mulholland reminded him that he had the same responsibilities as other staff members. In the elevator Chris was sometimes distracted by children on their way to interesting activities—he wanted to leave the elevator and join them. The antiquated, slow-moving elevator was hard to manipulate, and sometimes squabbles broke out when Chris took extra time to help severely handicapped students. But in time, Chris mastered these problems and became such a good operator that if he had stayed at P.S. 138, he probably would have eventually been promoted to a more demanding job.

Meanwhile, a writers' strike in Hollywood put Braverman's plans on hold. It was not until the strike was resolved in August 1988 that he was able to approach ABC executives with an idea for a family show built around Chris. By November, the script for the first episode was nearly done and Braverman called Marian to find out whether Chris could be available for the program. She said he could, but she and Braverman agreed to say nothing to Chris until plans about the show were firm. Two weeks later, after ABC had approved the script, Braverman called Chris to tell him the news and ask him to come to California for a meeting about the show, which would be called "Life Goes On."

"When can I be there?" was Chris's only question.

Chris and Frank flew to the West Coast. As of yet, no other cast members had been hired, so Chris read lines with

Deedee Bradley, the casting director. Bradley took the part of Drew Thacher, the father of Corky, whom Chris would be playing. After she read the line when Corky's father says, "When is the last time I told you how proud I am of you?" she looked up and saw tears in Chris's eyes, and she started crying, too. They went over to ABC to read again and choked up on the same lines, comforting each other with a hug at the end. A few minutes later Braverman told

A woodcut by Gustave Doré illustrates Edgar Allan Poe's classic poem, "The Raven." Chris had to memorize the first lines of "The Raven" and deliver them during a climactic moment in the first episode of "Life Goes On."

Chris he had the job. Once again, Chris was overjoyed, dancing down the hall shouting "I got it! I got it!"

Chris went back to New York and told his friends that he was going to be playing a teenager with Down syndrome on an ABC television series. At P.S. 138 people realized that Chris's dreams were about to come true.

During quiet times, Chris studied his part in the elevator. One day a friend boarded the elevator and saw Chris reading "The Raven," a poem by Edgar Allan Poe. The friend asked Chris if he was a Poe fan. "I have to learn this for my movie," Chris said.

"The Raven" is a tongue twister of a poem that begins:

> Once upon a midnight dreary,
> while I pondered, weak and weary,
> Over many a quaint and curious
> volume of forgotten lore—
> While I nodded, nearly napping,
> suddenly there came a tapping,
> As of some one gently rapping,
> rapping at my chamber door.

Chris's friend could not help wondering if Chris, with his stutter, his problems pronouncing sounds like *dr* and word endings like *ing,* and his unreliable memory would ever master the poem.

With the premiere of "Life Goes On" in 1989, Chris made history by becoming the first actor with Down syndrome to have a major role on a television series.

7

THE COVER OF LIFE

IN LOS ANGELES, on the night before the first rehearsal for "Life Goes On," Chris came down with a fever that blistered his face and tongue so badly he could not eat the steak he had ordered for dinner. Frank and Marian were worried that he would be unable to pronounce his lines the next day. But Marian rubbed the blisters with petroleum jelly and when Chris awoke the next morning they had disappeared.

Chris was eager to meet his costars in "Life Goes On." Bill Smitrovich, who would play Corky's father, was a veteran movie and television actor. He had appeared in several movies and on TV shows such as "Miami Vice." Smitrovich also had a degree in education with a minor in special education, and he had helped develop a workshop for mentally retarded people near his home in Connecticut, so he was an ideal person to work with Chris. They were comfortable with each other from the beginning. When he was asked about working with

Chris, Smitrovich said, "It requires a little more patience, to be truthful. But someone once said that [people with Down syndrome] have something extra, so I look at Corky as having something extra. . . . [Chris] works hard and we get it done. And sometimes there's a nice subtle variable in his character. He's able to add nuance to it, unlike other actors who are straight and playing someone retarded."

"Life Goes On" told the story of the Thacher family, played (from left to right) by Patti LuPone, Bill Smitrovich, Kellie Martin, Chris Burke, and Monique Lanier. Chris played the middle child, Corky Thacher.

Corky's mother would be played by Patti LuPone, the Tony Award–winning actress who had starred on Broadway in *Evita* and *Anything Goes.* LuPone was not only a musical comedy star but a dramatic actress as well. She was the first American ever to play a principal role with the Royal Shakespeare Company in England. Burke was thrilled to work with her. He had seen her perform on

Broadway, and he told her that he loved her performance. LuPone had never worked with anyone with a handicap and had misgivings about working with Burke, but when she met him and saw how warm he was, and when she heard him sing one of her songs from *Les Miserables,* she stopped worrying. "I had a sort of leeriness about it," she recalled. "But from the moment I met him, it was okay. He has such an outpouring of love. He has no pretense."

Kellie Martin, who was going to play Corky's precocious younger sister, Becca, was shocked when Michael Braverman told her that Burke's role, Corky Thacher, was going to be played by someone who actually had Down syndrome. When Chris came up to her and gave her a hug, she was a little afraid; but when he sat down to read his lines, she realized that he knew his part better than she knew hers, and she was impressed. "In the beginning, I never thought I'd warm up to him," she remembered. "But it naturally happens to everyone who knows Chris. He is so gentle, and loving, and he always wants you to feel comfortable."

For three weeks the cast and crew filmed the pilot episode, in which Corky's parents realize that, for financial reasons, they have to mainstream Corky in a public school—much to the disgust of his younger sister, who fears he is going to wreck her social life. Corky tries hard in school and does so well that a teacher accuses him of cheating. In the climax of the show, Corky is forced to prove his innocence by reciting "The Raven."

When it came time for Chris to recite the poem, the cast and crew became more and more nervous. If Burke could not carry his role, there would be no show. As the moment came, everyone waited behind the lights to see what would happen. The director called for action, cameras rolled, the actor who played the teacher delivered his accusation, and Chris recited:

Once upon a midnight dreary,
while I pondered, weak and weary . . .

When he finished, there was a moment of silence and then the crowd burst into applause. Chris remembered the moment with great pride, recalling that "Patti LuPone had tears in her eyes—real tears!" LuPone said afterward that she "simply wasn't prepared" for the impact of Burke's recitation. As she put it "He's fresh, he's desirous. What more can you want?"

After the pilot was finished, Chris and his parents flew back to New York. He returned to his job at P.S. 138 and waited to hear whether ABC would decide to shoot more episodes. There was a possibility that "Life Goes On" might have only one episode, as had happened with the pilot for "Desperate."

The ABC executives appreciated Burke's performance and they admired the show, but they still needed to select a time slot for the program. The Federal Communications Commission required that shows at 7:00 P.M. be either informational, sports-related, or family-oriented, and therefore 7:00 P.M. seemed like a natural time slot, one that would enable young children to watch. ABC executives did not expect "Life Goes On" to have blockbuster ratings because it was neither a comedy nor a crime show. Sunday at 7:00 P.M. seemed appropriate because the show would be running opposite "60 Minutes," which had been one of the highest rated shows on TV for years; even modest ratings in that time slot would be positive.

In May 1989, Michael Braverman called Chris to tell him that ABC had ordered 13 more episodes. He said that the show would air on Sundays and filming would start in July. Chris could hardly contain his excitement. His parents, on the other hand, were pleased about the opportunity but worried that Chris was giving up his steady, secure job at P.S. 138. They knew from the days when Ellen, Anne, and J. R. acted in commercials that success in show business can be fleeting. They consented, however, and Chris told the staff at P.S. 138 that he would be leaving his position at the school.

Suddenly Chris was inundated with requests for interviews. When a local TV station came to P.S. 138 to photograph him in his elevator, 20 people crowded onto the elevator to get into the picture. So many reporters wrote articles about Burke that the bulletin board at P.S. 138 became packed with clippings. Chris would be earning a six-figure salary, with Marian and Frank serving as his business managers, and J. R. as an unpaid financial adviser.

In July, by the time Frank and Chris had moved into a two-bedroom apartment in Los Angeles, reporters were lining up to interview Chris. He met with them in a trailer on the television set, and between interviews Frank tried to get Chris to take naps. (People with Down syndrome frequently get tired because of their limited muscle development.) But with all the excitement, Frank was not always successful in his efforts.

Father and son lived together much like the characters on the TV show "The Odd Couple," loving each other, appreciating each other's companionship, but often running into disputes. Frank was neat and Chris was messy. At home, Chris had always made his own breakfast, but in Los Angeles, because he had to be on the set early, Frank stepped in and made breakfast for him. In New York in the mornings, Chris liked to dawdle; in Los Angeles Frank had to get him started early in order to arrive at work on time. In the evenings, after a long day on the set, Chris wanted to relax, but Frank had to nag him into learning his lines. In time, though, they fell into a routine.

In the second episode of the program, Burke's character, Corky, gets a job as a baby-sitter. While he baby-sits, there is a gas leak and Corky has to lead his six-year-old charge and his puppy to safety. On the way, the boy and his puppy fall down a ravine and Corky has to rescue them while singing "Three Blind Mice" to ease the boy's fears.

A thick fog made by the special effects department filled the air and the summer night was sweltering as

On an episode of "Life Goes On" entitled "The Babysitter," Chris rescues a six-year-old boy, played by Jacob Gelman (right), from a ravine.

the crew filmed the rescue scene. The camera operator perched on a crane 30 feet in the air while the director and dialogue coach hung on ropes close to Chris to give him directions.

On the first take Chris sang a few bars of "Three Blind Mice" and then, instead of going to look for a rescue line hanging over the edge of the ravine, he said, "I'm back," a piece of dialogue that he was not supposed to deliver until he had returned with the line.

"You haven't left yet," the director said.

In the next scene Chris had to wiggle down the rescue line, grab the puppy, put it inside his jacket, lift the boy onto his back, and crawl up the line. During the first take he had plenty of energy, but the hot night, the heavy jacket, and the repeated takes took their toll. By the time Frank got Chris home and in bed that night, Chris was so exhausted that Frank wondered whether he could handle the part.

The cast and crew had their doubts as well. Sometimes Chris had trouble following directions. On the set, with the endless repetition of takes and the crew constantly giving him different commands ("Look here!" "Move left!" "Talk slowly!"), Chris easily became flustered—and when he was flustered, he stuttered.

His dialogue coach, Kaley Hummel, tried to help him prepare for scenes by talking about motivation, filling in the blanks between spoken lines. But nothing could change the fact that Chris's mouth was small and his tongue lacked muscle tone, which resulted in Chris slurring his words or getting stuck on letters such as *r*. Sometimes the writers had to rewrite lines to make it easier for him. "The word 'railroad' was changed to 'train set' because *r*'s are hard for him," recalled Hummel. "Conjunctions are hard, too."

Burke did most of his own action scenes without a double, but one day he had to play a scene in which he ran upstairs in front of a 750-pound pig. Chris was looking forward to doing the scene, but his father was worried that the pig might trample Chris on the stairs. Then it turned out that Sugar, the pig, was not very good at running up stairs, so a stunt pig was found to replace her. It was a fun scene and went smoothly.

As Burke learned the ropes of acting and became more comfortable on the set, some staff members realized that they had been babying him unnecessarily. The show's writers went to Chris and Frank to ask for ideas and were surprised to find that Chris could swim and ride a bike. An

Kaley Hummel (left), Chris's dialogue coach for "Life Goes On," helped Chris prepare for each scene. Hummel grew to admire Chris's positive attitude on the set. "Most actors are so judgmental of themselves, especially if a scene doesn't go well. But he can let it go better than anyone I've ever seen."

episode in which Corky enters a bike race became one of the most popular episodes of "Life Goes On" and was Chris's favorite.

Before the show aired on TV in September, *TV Guide* forecast an early death for it. "It's a family situation with its trials and tribulations," an advertising executive said in the article. "There is no new hook other than one of the children has Down syndrome—which isn't upbeat. It is well done, but I don't think Middle America will want to consistently tune in to it."

To expose as many viewers as possible to the first episode, ABC broadcast it on a Tuesday evening after the hit comedy show "Roseanne." The premiere of "Life Goes

Chris rests on the set with Bruce Pasternack, his favorite cameraman. The grueling shooting schedule forced Chris to learn to conserve his energy, but he adjusted to life on the set and before long he had become a seasoned veteran.

On" passed without much note by cast and crew because they had already seen the tape, but a few days later, when the ratings came in, they were ecstatic to find the show listed in the week's top 10.

Reviews of the first episode were excellent. Critics hailed the show's warmth and realism. *New York Times* television critic John J. O'Connor called it "sensitively written, wonderfully cast and beautifully executed . . . in the admirable family-drama tradition of 'The Waltons' and 'Family.'" Chris, himself an avid TV watcher, gave it a good review. "This is the best television show I've ever seen," he said. "And I watch a lot of television." Almost overnight, Chris became a celebrity. Chris and his parents were interviewed by *People Weekly,* the *New York Times,* and the *Washington Post.* When the cast of the show went out to lunch, people approached him for autographs, telling him that he was going to be a big star. Letters poured in from across the country, many from people who had some experience with Down syndrome. Chris and Frank tried to answer all of the letters personally.

Never content to bask in stardom, Burke seized every chance to educate people about the need for more opportunities for people with Down syndrome. Despite his grueling schedule during the week, he would often fly to other cities on weekends to give speeches or appear at charity functions. The Burkes were happy to have the opportunity to assist organizations and schools that were helping the disabled. "They were there when we needed them, so we wanted to be there for them," Frank said. "We didn't look at these as a chore. We looked at it as a commitment we couldn't avoid. We realize Chris is an inspiration to a lot of families. It's time to give something back."

Chris surprised many people with his passion and power as a speaker. He spoke earnestly and sincerely about his belief that all people with disabilities deserve respect and the chance to show what they could do. That a person with

In 1989, Chris delivered the keynote speech at the National Down Syndrome Congress in Denver, Colorado. Paul Wolff (rear), a writer for "Life Goes On" who accompanied Chris to the conference, said, "This may sound mystical, but it became clear to me that weekend that Chris Burke was prepared for this. He had just the right parents. He was the one who could break through and do this televison show, and bring these people the dignity they deserved, the chances they had deserved, and do it brilliantly."

Down syndrome was speaking not as a victim but as someone concerned with helping those less fortunate than himself made his point even more convincing.

When "Life Goes On" was put in its regular time slot on Sunday at 7:00 P.M., it was clobbered in the ratings. Out of 100 shows on the air, it was in the bottom 20. Cast and crew fell into a state of depression and assumed that the show was about to be canceled. But ABC executives had never expected "Life Goes On" to have high ratings, competing as it was against "60 Minutes." They were aiming for a small but relatively well-educated and affluent audience, which would be attractive to advertisers. They were more than satisfied when the show developed a loyal following, advertisers bought time, and the cost of ads began to climb. The network ordered nine more episodes to fill out the season.

In October 1989, Jack Egan, a cousin of the Burkes who worked in a printing plant was checking the press run of the next month's issue of *Life* when he stopped, thunderstruck. There, on the cover of *Life* magazine, was a picture of Chris Burke and Patti LuPone.

In November 1990, Chris Burke joined President George Bush at the White House to film a public service announcement about Down syndrome. He encountered Bush again at a banquet in Washington (behind them is actress Patricia Neal). When the Secret Service tried to block Burke's approach to the president, Bush told them, "It's okay, this is my friend Chris Burke."

8

President George

AFTER CHRIS APPEARED on the cover of *Life,* he was besieged by children asking for autographs wherever he went. One night in New York, the composer for "Life Goes On," Craig Safan, who has a child of his own with Down syndrome, was having dinner in a restaurant with the Burkes when a crowd of children came to their table seeking autographs. Safan was amazed to see that these children regarded Chris not as a handicapped person but as a star. "To see that kids have that view toward a retarded man is amazing," Safan said.

When he was in New York, Chris was followed in the street and was greeted from passing buses. (In Los Angeles, where many more movie and TV stars reside, people were more casual about spotting him.) Safan could see the effect Chris's achievements had had on his own child. One day he and his son were shopping in a sporting goods store when a teenager who worked there yelled, "Hey, he's like that little guy Corky on TV." The teenager grinned and threw Safan's son a ball. Safan feels that "Life Goes On" has made encounters such as this possible. "The show made it okay to be friendly with these kids," Safan said.

In November 1990, President George Bush invited Chris to join him at the White House to film a public service announcement about Down syndrome. The Burkes gathered at a hotel in Washington, D.C., where a limousine picked them up to take them to the White House.

As soon as they arrived, Chris was whisked away by an aide to have makeup applied for the cameras while the rest of the family was taken to the Diplomatic Reception Room. There they saw the presidential china, ranging from George Washington's simple blue and white dinner dishes to the Reagans' lavishly decorated red and gold porcelain. From the room's window they saw the sloping White House lawn, the Washington Monument, and the Jefferson Memorial. Everyone was awed except Frank, who was greeted by a Secret Service agent who remembered him from the days when Frank used to provide police security for presidential visits to New York City. When Chris returned, he found his father happily talking shop with the agents.

The family was hustled into a hall by security men and aides, who apologized for the delay, saying that the president had been detained because the Berlin Wall, the barrier between East and West Germany, had fallen, perhaps leading to the reunification of Germany. The Burkes had been guests at the White House on one of the most historic days of the 20th century.

When President Bush arrived, he and the Burkes walked outside to be interviewed for CBS's "Entertainment Tonight." President Bush expressed his concern for people with Down syndrome and his admiration for Chris. Afterward the president led the Burkes over to the White House fence, where he shook hands with some surprised—and

Flanked by his parents, Chris proudly accepts an award from the U.S. Junior Chamber of Commerce, which named him one of 10 outstanding young Americans in July 1991.

delighted—tourists who had been waiting in line for a tour of the White House. Suddenly, the president gave a yell and his two dogs came tearing over.

While the Burkes were patting the dogs, Marian mentioned that she was an admirer of the president's wife, Barbara. President Bush responded, "Well, you'll have to come up and meet her." He then took the Burkes upstairs to the First Lady's dressing room, where Barbara Bush, who had just been swimming, was having her hair done. Jokingly, the First Lady made Chris promise not to tell anyone that she had something as fancy as a private hairdresser. "This will be our secret, Chris," she said.

President Bush took Burke alone to his private office where they traded photographs and autographs and talked about their shared interest in country music. Chris's family later commented that when they came to meet him, Chris was calling the president George, but Chris denies this.

"We were in awe the whole time," Marian recalled. "But Chris took it all so naturally, like he met the president every day." The family had a private tour of the White

House and lunched in a private dining room. "The whole thing was so amazing," said Marian. "We have gone from the depth of despair, when Chris was born, to heights of unbelievable experiences like this. Chris has opened doors for us that we would never have gone through."

In January 1991, Burke was nominated for a Golden Globe award for best supporting actor in a dramatic series. He received many other awards, including Youth in Film's Inspiration to Youth Award and the St. Genesius medal for outstanding achievement in the entertainment business. He was named one of 10 outstanding young Americans by the U.S. Junior Chamber of Commerce and became a spokesman for the National Down Syndrome Congress and for the McDonald's McJobs program, which trains and employs people with disabilities.

In April 1991, "Life Goes On" was renewed for another season. When Chris returned to New York, the first thing he did was go back to visit P.S. 138, where he found a young retarded man operating his old elevator. Frank felt that this was one of Chris's greatest achievements; his success had led to "the opening of doors for others with handicaps."

Within minutes Chris was back in Tom Roeder's classroom. The students were not the children he knew from the year before; they were all new. Most were severely retarded and had no idea who Burke was. But he did not care. He got down on his knees and hugged them and played with them, and it seemed as though he had never left. A few days later Burke and Roeder had lunch at their favorite restaurant, ordering bacon, eggs, and fries as usual, expecting to joke like they always had, but the restaurant soon filled with so many fans that Chris became frightened. The noise and the press of bodies reminded him that John Lennon had been killed by a disturbed fan. "I like meeting my fans," he said later, "but not when it's scary."

Tom Roeder knew from his visits to New York City schools how important Burke was to children. Part of

Chris surprised his co-workers by learning to surf for an episode of "Life Goes On" set in Hawaii. As the show's writers learned more about Chris, they discovered unsuspected talents that they could incorporate into their scripts. When they learned he could ride a bicycle, for example, they wrote an episode in which Corky enters a bike race.

Roeder's job was to go from school to school to tell people about mainstreaming. One of Roeder's goals was to help children respect people with disabilities, but he discovered that Burke, who had high visibility with children, had already done much of his work. Whenever he asked if anyone had seen Chris in "Life Goes On," all the children would raise their hands. He would then talk about how Chris was limited in certain ways, but gifted in others. This would lead to a discussion of how all children have gifts and how it is important to find these gifts and respect them.

One of the biggest reasons for Burke's success as an actor is that he expresses feelings that everyone, disabled or not, has felt at one time or another. As director Rick Rosenthal put it, "What kid growing up in America really thinks he or she is normal? When Chris is at his best, he lets us in emotionally. He has a wonderfully expressive face. He's able to show the emotions of what so many people feel about being different. Very few actors, very few characters on television can do that."

"Life Goes On" writer Michael Nankin said the character of Corky is meant to convey this message of understanding and acceptance. "He's a well-meaning outcast who wants nothing more than to fit in and be accepted and be loved. Everyone can identify with that."

When their vacation was over and the "Life Goes On" cast and crew gathered in Hawaii to shoot the first two episodes of the new season, they were impressed by how much Burke had changed. Michael Braverman said that Chris had grown in every way as an actor. "The concentration it requires, the discipline it requires, the focus it requires—he has grown in all those areas." (People with Down syndrome develop longer than others. They often keep improving their reading skills and math skills well into their twenties.)

The new shows touched on a subject that had formerly been taboo—the sexuality of people with Down syndrome. In "Life Goes On," Corky's first encounter with sex is in an episode called "Corky's Travels" in which Corky gets lost in a rainstorm and is taken home by a young prostitute. The prostitute asks Corky whether he has ever gone beyond kissing, and Corky says no. She asks whether he ever thinks about sex and he says, "All the time." She then gives him a tender look and turns off the light.

David Wolf, the episode's writer, said, "To me, it's interesting about these people we regard as childlike, but other parts of them work on the same levels as everyone else. A normal teenage boy is widely preoccupied with sex. It's something we barely touch on in the show. It's a very human side of him that can get lost. It's another way in which his emotions are not far from those we all experience."

The Burkes were upset when they read the script for the episode, but they decided that it was better to bring the subject of sexuality out into the open. People with Down syndrome are often seen as perpetual children, when in truth they have as much interest in sex as anyone else. The

Burkes knew it was important to remind people that Chris deserved to be seen as an adult. "The main thing was the part with the hooker," said Marian. "That was a little rough for us." Chris handled the situation well. He was nervous when shooting began, but as it got under way he began to enjoy it, especially the kissing.

"Life Goes On" was renewed for two more seasons, during which it explored the theme of intimate relations even further. In the third season Corky has a romantic encounter with a girl with cerebral palsy. Later he falls in love with Amanda Swanson (played by Andrea Friedman)

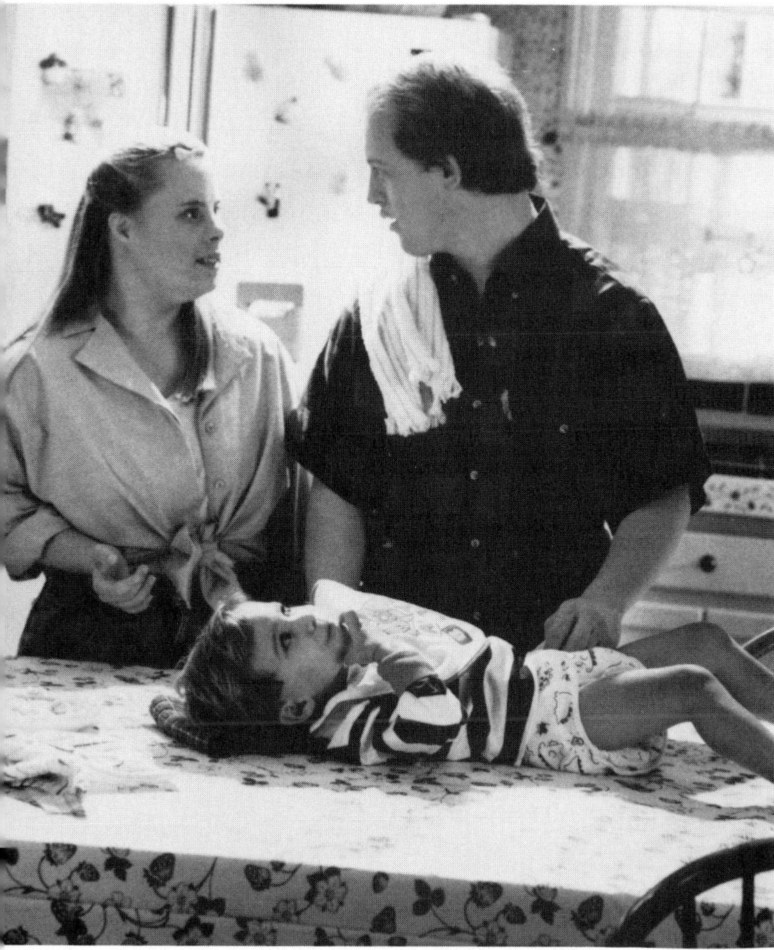

In an episode of "Life Goes On" that explored the issue of adult relationships between people with Down syndrome, Corky and Amanda (Burke and Andrea Friedman) prepare for marriage by taking care of Corky's infant brother, Nick.

a woman with Down syndrome who is a student at Santa Monica College. In the fourth season the romance between Corky and Amanda has rocky moments. In one episode, Corky's parents become angry because they think he has gone too far too quickly in his relationship with Amanda. In another they react with relief when it seems as if Corky and Amanda have given up their wedding plans. (People with Down syndrome marry more frequently today than they used to, and they often live in group homes that give them a combination of independence and support. Birth control is an important issue for these couples because one out of every two babies born to women with Down syndrome has the syndrome.)

The show ran through half of the fourth season and was canceled in early 1993. Through that time Burke's skill as an actor continued to grow. "When I started doing this show," said Bill Smitrovich, "I thought of Chris as a kid with Down syndrome who wanted to be an actor. Now I think of him as an actor who just happens to have Down syndrome."

Some of Burke's associates were concerned about how he would handle the end of the series. In the summer of 1992, when the show was still on the air, the Burkes had a chance encounter with the co-executive producer of the program, Bob Goodwin, in Cambria, California, and they decided to have dinner together. During the meal, the conversation turned serious. Goodwin wanted to make sure that Chris would not be taken by surprise if the series was canceled, and he asked him how he would handle it. "You understand the show won't go on forever," he told Chris.

Burke leaned back, took a swig of his Coke, and said, "Well, Bob—I guess life goes off."

The cancellation of "Life Goes On" after four successful seasons definitely did not mean the end of an acting career for Burke, who had already been pursuing guest appearances on other shows for years. In 1992, Chris

In October 1992, Burke and JoBeth Williams starred in a television movie, "Jonathan: The Boy Nobody Wanted." Based on a true story, the movie concerns a hospital volunteer who befriends a boy with Down syndrome. When his parents try to withhold a lifesaving operation, preferring to let their son die, the volunteer sues to become his legal guardian.

starred in "Jonathan: The Boy Nobody Wanted," broadcast on "NBC Monday Night at the Movies" on October 19. Based on a true story, the film showed the relationship between a boy with Down syndrome, Jonathan Willis, played by Burke, and a volunteer at the institution where he lives, Ginny Moore, played by JoBeth Williams. Moore befriends Jonathan and attempts to improve his relation-

In June 1993, Chris Burke and Joe DeMasi perform songs from their album Lollipops and Love Songs *at an elementary school in Staten Island, New York. Burke has made several visits to schools and nursing homes with folksingers John and Joe DeMasi.*

ship with his family. But when Jonathan's parents refuse to consent to a potentially lifesaving operation because they consider him a burden on the family, Moore fights to become his legal guardian.

Burke's agent, Harry Abrams, is very optimistic about Chris's future. "His career is made, as far as I'm concerned. . . . I think it shocked a lot of people that he could hold up to the rigors of a show. The TV creative public will remember him for years to come."

By age 27, Burke had achieved his professional goals: he had become a star and he had performed on his own TV series. He was a millionaire before the age of 30. "Life

Goes On" had been shown in Australia, Bermuda, Bolivia, Bophuthatswana, Brunei, Canada, Chile, Colombia, Costa Rica, Finland, Germany, Greece, Holland, Indonesia, Ireland, Italy, Japan, Kenya, Kuwait, Luxembourg, Malaysia, Malta, Mexico, Namibia, New Zealand, Panama, Peru, the Philippines, Portugal, Puerto Rico, South Africa, Spain, Taiwan, Thailand, Turkey, the United Kingdom, Venezuela and Zimbabwe.

In 1991, Burke wrote a book, with reporter Jo Beth McDaniel, about the story of his life. *A Special Kind of Hero* received excellent reviews and was recommended by the National Down Syndrome Society as a good way to learn about the syndrome and the capacities of people who have it.

In 1993, a German television station bought the rights to air two years of episodes of "Life Goes On," and Chris and his parents were invited to tour Germany to help promote the show. They visited Bonn, Munich, Düsseldorf, Cologne, and Hamburg. Always eager to lend a hand to organizations promoting rights for the disabled, they combined their tour with a visit to the Down syndrome society in Barcelona, Spain, thus saving the organization the expense of flying them to Europe. They spent a week in Barcelona, where Chris gave speeches calling for more opportunities for the disabled.

Also in 1993, Burke landed parts on two major television programs. First he performed as a guest star on the one-hour police drama "The Commish," in which he played a leading role as Billy, a person with Down syndrome who witnesses a murder. As the key to the prosecutor's case, he has to endure ridicule from the defendant's lawyer and skepticism from those who doubt the reliability of his testimony, including the judge. Billy's strength and courage are further tested when his apartment is ransacked and his dog, Ginger, is stolen. Billy refuses to back down, and with his help the criminal is brought to justice.

Burke next appeared in the miniseries "Heaven and Hell," the conclusion of John Jakes's *North and South* trilogy of historical novels. "Heaven and Hell," which aired in early 1994, takes place in the aftermath of the Civil War during the Reconstruction era. The part called for Chris to ride a horse, and he prepared by taking riding lessons at the Red Barn Riding Stables in Old Brookville, Long Island, in New York. (The Burkes had moved back to New York City after Chris finished filming his last episode of "Life Goes On" in California.) Frank Burke said that Chris enjoyed working on "Heaven and Hell" a great deal. "He got to dress in dirty old western outfits, ride

The Burke family celebrates Thanksgiving in 1992. Marian and Frank Burke are seated in front of Chris (center). Behind Chris stand J. R. and his wife, Betsy. In front of Betsy is Chris's sister Anne; his other sister, Ellen, is seated at the lower right, holding her daughter Nora. Ellen's husband, Jack Orlando, stands at the far right.

a horse, lead a pack mule, and then he gets killed by Plains Indians."

Burke fulfilled another longtime dream when he made a recording with the DeMasi brothers entitled *Lollipops and Love Songs.* The cassette was marketed to schools and nursing homes with an accompanying workbook, and Burke and the DeMasis visited institutions to perform songs from the tape.

But Burke's main goal has always been simple. "What I wanted to do ever since I was a little tyke, was to let people know that the inside of me is just like everyone else." Handicapped people "have dreams and hopes and ambitions," Chris said. "We laugh and have fun, and we can be serious and do a good job. We can do lots of things if people give us the chance."

FURTHER READING

Burke, Chris, and Jo Beth McDaniel. *A Special Kind of Hero.* New York: Doubleday, 1991.

Hanson, Marci J. *Teaching the Infant with Down Syndrome.* Austin, TX: Pro Ed Publishers, 1987.

Kingsley, Jason, and Michael Levitz. *Count Us In: Growing Up with Down Syndrome.* Orlando, FL: Harcourt Brace Jovanovich, 1994.

Nadel, Lynn, ed. *The Psychobiology of Down Syndrome.* Cambridge, MA: MIT Press, 1988.

Pueschel, Siegfried M. *A Parent's Guide to Down Syndrome.* Baltimore, MD: Paul H. Brooks, 1990.

VIDEOS

(Video rentals are sometimes available from the producers.)

Gifts of Love. Produced by and available from the National Down Syndrome Society, 666 Broadway, Suite 810, New York, NY, 10012; 800-221-4602.

Opportunities To Grow. Produced by and available from the National Down Syndrome Society.

Special Days with Special Kids. Produced by the Association for Children with Down Syndrome, Inc., 2616 Martin Avenue, Bellmore, NY, 11710; 516-221-4700.

CASSETTE

Lollipops and Love Songs. Fourteen songs for kids ages eight and younger performed by Chris Burke and Joe and John DeMasi. Includes an activity book. Produced by Joe and John DeMasi and available from C.J.J. Enterprises, P.O. Box 9854, Coral Springs, FL, 33075.

FURTHER INFORMATION

The National Down Syndrome Society *(see above for address)*

The National Down Syndrome Congress
1800 Dempster Street
Park Ridge, IL 60068-1146
800-232-6372

Association for Retarded Citizens
P.O. Box 1047
Arlington, TX 76004
817-261-6003

CHRONOLOGY

1965	Born Christopher Joseph Burke on August 26 in New York City
1968	Begins speech therapy
1969	Enters Kennedy Child Study Center in New York City
1971	Decides to become an actor after performing in a play at age five
1973	Graduates from Kennedy Child Study Center; enters Cardinal Cushing School in Hanover, Massachusetts
1978	Enters Don Guanella school in Springfield, Pennsylvania
1983	Gets summer maintenance job at a park in Point Lookout, Long Island
1985	Sees Jason Kingsley on episode of "The Fall Guy"; begins correspondence with Jason's mother, Emily
1986	Graduates from Don Guanella school; gets call from Warner Brothers Studio inviting him to audition for television series
1987	Appears in television movie "Desperate," but series is not picked up by ABC
1988	Gets paid staff position at New York City's P.S. 138 in February, becoming the first person with a mental disability to be hired by the school district; offered part in "Life Goes On" in November
1989	"Life Goes On" premieres; Chris is featured in *People Weekly,* the *New York Times,* the *Washington Post,* and on the cover of *Life*
1990	Meets President George Bush and films public service announcement at the White House
1991	Nominated for Golden Globe Award; voted one of ten Outstanding Young Americans by U.S. Junior Chamber of Commerce; becomes spokesman for the National Down Syndrome Congress and for the McDonald's McJobs program; coauthors *A Special Kind of Hero* with Jo Beth McDaniel
1992	"Life Goes On" renewed for fourth season; stars in television movie "Jonathan: The Boy Nobody Wanted"; records *Lollipops and Love Songs* with John and Joe DeMasi
1993	"Life Goes On" canceled; tours Germany and Spain
1994	Guest stars on episode of "The Commish"; appears in television miniseries "Heaven and Hell"; regularly edits the National Down Syndrome Society's newsletter

INDEX

PICTURE CREDITS

AP/Wide World Photos: pp. 40, 72; The Bettmann Archive: p. 80; Courtesy of the Burke family: pp. 2, 12, 15, 20, 26, 28, 36, 38, 46, 48, 50, 53, 55, 58, 60, 66, 69, 75, 89, 90, 92, 94, 99, 106; © 1994 Capital Cities/ABC, Inc.: p. 77; Courtesy of Joe and John DeMasi: pp. 16–17; Courtesy of Don Guanella school: p. 62; National Library of Medicine: pp. 31, 33; Photofest: pp. 42, 82, 84, 88, 101, 103; Reuters/Bettmann: p. 67; Courtesy of Tom Roeder: p. 23; *Staten Island Advance,* Photo by Jan Somma: p. 104; Courtesy of the United States Junior Chamber of Commerce: p. 97.

Helen Monsoon Geraghty has written about children and families for *Family Circle, Child, Sesame Street Magazine,* and *Sesame Street Parents Newsletter.* She graduated cum laude from Radcliffe College in Massachusetts and earned a masters degree in early childhood education from Teachers College, Columbia University, in New York City. Geraghty's experience with children with special needs includes running a day care center, after school program, and summer camp at the Riverdale Neighborhood House, which offered services to mainstreamed children, and at Googolplex, a school for preschoolers that she founded and directed. As a consultant for the Brooklyn College Daycare Training Project, she trained day care professionals to help integrate children with special needs into their classrooms. She lives in New York City with her daughter, Maisie, and her dog, Jazzie.

ACKNOWLEDGEMENTS

The author and publisher wish to thank Marian, Frank, and Chris Burke for their generous help in reviewing the manuscript and in loaning family photographs for reproduction in this book.

Jerry Lewis is the National Chairman of the Muscular Dystrophy Association (MDA) and host of the MDA Labor Day Telethon. An internationally acclaimed comedian, Lewis began his entertainment career in New York and then performed in a comedy team with singer and actor Dean Martin from 1946 to 1956. Lewis has appeared in many films—including *The Delicate Delinquent, Rock a Bye Baby, The Bellboy, Cinderfella, The Nutty Professor, The Disorderly Orderly,* and *The King of Comedy*—and his comedy performances continue to delight audiences around the world.

John Callahan is a nationally syndicated cartoonist and the author of an illustrated autobiography, *Don't Worry, He Won't Get Far on Foot.* He has also produced three cartoon collections: *Do Not Disturb Any Further, Digesting the Child Within,* and *Do What He Says! He's Crazy!!!* He has recently been the subject of feature articles in the *New York Times Magazine,* the *Los Angeles Times Magazine,* and the Cleveland *Plain Dealer,* and has been profiled on "60 Minutes." Callahan resides in Portland, Oregon.